Alexander's Bridge and
The Barrel Organ

Willa Cather and Alfred Noyes

Contents

ALEXANDER'S BRIDGE AND THE BARREL ORGAN

BY

Willa Cather and Alfred Noyes

CHAPTER I

L ate one brilliant April afternoon Professor Lucius Wilson stood at the head of Chestnut Street, looking about him with the pleased air of a man of taste who does not very often get to Boston. He had lived there as a student, but for twenty years and more, since he had been Professor of Philosophy in a Western university, he had seldom come East except to take a steamer for some foreign port. Wilson was standing quite still, contemplating with a whimsical smile the slanting street, with its worn paving, its irregular, gravely colored houses, and the row of naked trees on which the thin sunlight was still shining. The gleam of the river at the foot of the hill made him blink a little, not so much because it was too bright as because he found it so pleasant. The few passers-by glanced at him unconcernedly, and even the children who hurried along with their school-bags under their arms seemed to find it perfectly natural that a tall brown gentleman should be standing there, looking up through his glasses at the gray housetops.

The sun sank rapidly; the silvery light had faded from the bare boughs and the watery twilight was setting in when Wilson at last walked down the hill, descending into cooler and cooler depths of grayish shadow. His nostril, long unused to it, was quick to detect the smell of wood smoke in the air, blended with the odor of moist spring earth and the saltiness that came up the river with the tide. He crossed Charles Street between jangling street cars and shelving lumber drays, and after a moment of uncertainty wound into Brimmer Street. The street was quiet, deserted, and hung with a thin bluish haze. He had already fixed his sharp eye upon the house which he reasoned should be his objective point, when he noticed a woman approaching rapidly from the opposite direction. Always an interested observer of women, Wilson would have slackened his pace anywhere to follow this one with his impersonal, appreciative glance. She was a person of distinction he saw at once, and, moreover, very handsome. She was tall, carried her beautiful head proudly, and moved with ease and certainty. One immediately took for granted the costly privileges and fine spaces that must lie in the background from which such a figure could emerge with this rapid and elegant gait. Wilson noted her dress, too,--for, in his way, he had an eye for such things,--particularly her brown furs and her hat. He got a blurred impression of her fine color, the violets she wore, her white gloves, and, curiously enough, of her veil, as she turned up a flight of steps in front of him and disappeared.

Wilson was able to enjoy lovely things that passed him on the wing as completely and deliberately as if they had been dug-up marvels, long anticipated, and definitely fixed at the end of a railway journey. For a few pleasurable seconds he quite forgot where he was going, and only after the door had closed behind her did he realize that the young woman had entered the house to which he had directed his trunk from the South Station that morning. He hesitated a moment before mounting the steps. "Can that," he murmured in amazement,--"can that possibly have been Mrs. Alexander?"

When the servant admitted him, Mrs. Alexander was still standing in the hallway. She heard him give his name, and came forward holding out her hand.

"Is it you, indeed, Professor Wilson? I was afraid that you might get here before I did. I was detained at a concert, and Bartley telephoned that he would be late. Thomas will show you your room. Had you rather have your tea brought to you there, or will you have it down here with me, while we wait for Bartley?"

Wilson was pleased to find that he had been the cause of her rapid walk, and with her he was even more vastly pleased than before. He followed her through the drawing-room into the library, where the wide back windows looked out upon the garden and the sunset and a fine stretch of silver-colored river. A harp-shaped elm stood stripped against the pale-colored evening sky, with ragged last year's birds' nests in its forks, and through the bare branches the evening star quivered in the misty air. The long brown room breathed the peace of a rich and amply guarded quiet. Tea was brought in immediately and placed in front of the wood fire. Mrs. Alexander sat down in a high-backed chair and began to pour it, while Wilson sank into a low seat opposite her and took his cup with a great sense of ease and harmony and comfort.

"You have had a long journey, haven't you?" Mrs. Alexander asked, after showing gracious concern about his tea. "And I am so sorry Bartley is late. He's often tired when he's late. He flatters himself that it is a little on his account that you have come to this Congress of Psychologists."

"It is," Wilson assented, selecting his muffin carefully; "and I hope he won't be tired tonight. But, on my own account, I'm glad to have a few moments alone with you, before Bartley comes. I was somehow afraid that my knowing him so well would not put me in the way of getting to know you."

"That's very nice of you." She nodded at him above her cup and smiled, but there was a little formal tightness in her tone which had not been there when she greeted him in the hall.

Wilson leaned forward. "Have I said something awkward? I live very far out of the world, you know. But I didn't mean that you would exactly fade dim, even if Bartley were here."

Mrs. Alexander laughed relentingly. "Oh, I'm not so vain! How terribly discerning you are."

She looked straight at Wilson, and he felt that this quick, frank glance brought about an understanding between them.

He liked everything about her, he told himself, but he particularly liked her eyes; when she looked at one directly for a moment they were like a glimpse of fine windy sky that may bring all sorts of weather.

"Since you noticed something," Mrs. Alexander went on, "it must have been a flash of the distrust I have come to feel whenever I meet any of the people who knew Bartley when he was a boy. It is always as if they were talking of someone I had never met. Really, Professor Wilson, it would seem that he grew up among the strangest people. They usually say that he has turned out very well, or remark that he always was a fine fellow. I never know what reply to make."

Wilson chuckled and leaned back in his chair, shaking his left foot gently. "I expect the fact is that we none of us knew him very well, Mrs. Alexander. Though I will say for myself that I was always confident he'd do something extraordinary."

Mrs. Alexander's shoulders gave a slight movement, suggestive of impatience. "Oh, I should think that might have been a safe prediction. Another cup, please?"

"Yes, thank you. But predicting, in the case of boys, is not so easy as you might imagine, Mrs. Alexander. Some get a bad hurt early and lose their courage; and some never get a fair wind. Bartley"--he dropped his chin on the back of his long hand and looked at her admiringly--"Bartley caught the wind early, and it has sung in his sails ever since."

Mrs. Alexander sat looking into the fire with intent preoccupation, and Wilson studied her half-averted face. He liked the suggestion of stormy possibilities in the proud curve of her lip and nostril. Without that, he reflected, she would be too cold.

"I should like to know what he was really like when he was a boy. I don't believe he remembers," she said suddenly. "Won't you smoke, Mr. Wilson?"

Wilson lit a cigarette. "No, I don't suppose he does. He was never introspective. He was simply the most tremendous response to stimuli I have ever known. We didn't know exactly what to do with him."

A servant came in and noiselessly removed the tea-tray. Mrs. Alexander screened her face from the firelight, which was beginning to throw wavering bright spots on her dress and hair as the dusk deepened.

"Of course," she said, "I now and again hear stories about things that happened when he was in college."

"But that isn't what you want." Wilson wrinkled his brows and looked at her with the smiling familiarity that had come about so quickly. "What you want is a picture of him, standing back there at the other end of twenty years. You want to look down through my memory."

She dropped her hands in her lap. "Yes, yes; that's exactly what I want."

At this moment they heard the front door shut with a jar, and Wilson laughed as Mrs. Alexander rose quickly. "There he is. Away with perspective! No past, no future for Bartley; just the fiery moment. The only moment that ever was or will be in the world!"

The door from the hall opened, a voice called "Winifred?" hurriedly, and a big man came through the drawing-room with a quick, heavy tread, bringing with him a smell of cigar smoke and chill out-of-doors air. When Alexander reached the library door, he switched on the lights and stood six feet and more in the archway, glowing with strength and cordiality and rugged, blond good looks. There were other bridge-builders in the world, certainly, but it was always Alexander's picture that the Sunday Supplement men wanted, because he looked as a tamer of rivers ought to look. Under his tumbled sandy hair his head seemed as hard and powerful as a catapult, and his shoulders looked strong enough in themselves to support a span of any one of his ten great bridges that cut the air above as many rivers.

After dinner Alexander took Wilson up to his study. It was a large room over the library, and looked out upon the black river and the row of white lights along the Cambridge Embankment. The room was not at all what one might expect of an engineer's study. Wilson felt at once the harmony of beautiful things that have lived long together without obtrusions of ugliness or change. It was none of Alexander's doing, of course; those warm consonances of color had been blending and mellowing before he was born. But the wonder was that he was not out of place there,--that it all seemed to glow like the inevitable background for his vigor and vehemence. He sat before the fire, his shoulders deep in the cushions of his chair, his powerful head upright, his hair rumpled above his broad forehead. He sat heavily, a cigar in his large, smooth hand, a flush of after-dinner color in his face, which wind and sun and exposure to all sorts of weather had left fair and clear-skinned.

"You are off for England on Saturday, Bartley, Mrs. Alexander tells me."

"Yes, for a few weeks only. There's a meeting of British engineers, and I'm doing another bridge in Canada, you know."

"Oh, every one knows about that. And it was in Canada that you met your wife, wasn't it?"

"Yes, at Allway. She was visiting her great-aunt there. A most remarkable old lady. I was working with MacKeller then, an old Scotch engineer who had picked me up in London and taken me back to Quebec with him. He had the contract for the Allway Bridge, but before he began work on it he found out that he was going to die, and he advised the committee to turn the job over to me. Otherwise I'd never have got anything good so early. MacKeller was an old friend of Mrs. Pemberton, Winifred's aunt. He had mentioned me to her, so when I went to Allway she asked me to come to see her. She was a wonderful old lady."

"Like her niece?" Wilson queried.

Bartley laughed. "She had been very handsome, but not in Winifred's way. When I knew her she was little and fragile, very pink and white, with a splendid head and a face like fine old lace, somehow,--but perhaps I always think of that because she wore a lace scarf on her hair. She had such a flavor of life about her. She had known Gordon and Livingstone and Beaconsfield when she was young,--every one. She was the first woman of that sort I'd ever known. You know how it is in the West,--old people are poked out of the way. Aunt Eleanor fascinated me as few young women have ever done. I used to go up from the works to have tea with her, and sit talking to her for hours. It was very stimulating, for she couldn't tolerate stupidity."

"It must have been then that your luck began, Bartley," said Wilson, flicking his cigar ash with his long finger. "It's curious, watching boys," he went on reflectively. "I'm sure I did you justice in the matter of ability. Yet I always used to feel that there was a weak spot where some day strain would tell. Even after you began to climb, I stood down in the crowd and watched you with--well, not with confidence. The more dazzling the front you presented, the higher your facade rose, the more I expected to see a big crack zigzagging from top to bottom,"--he indicated its course in the air with his forefinger,--"then a crash and clouds of dust. It was curious. I had such a clear picture of it. And another curious thing, Bartley," Wilson spoke with deliberateness and settled deeper into his chair, "is that I don't feel it any longer. I am sure of you."

Alexander laughed. "Nonsense! It's not I you feel sure of; it's Winifred. People often make that mistake."

"No, I'm serious, Alexander. You've changed. You have decided to leave some birds in the bushes. You used to want them all."

Alexander's chair creaked. "I still want a good many," he said rather gloomily. "After all, life doesn't offer a man much. You work like the devil and think you're getting on, and suddenly you discover that you've only been getting yourself tied up. A million details drink you dry. Your life keeps going for things you don't want, and all the while you are being built alive into a social structure you don't care a rap about. I sometimes wonder what sort of chap I'd have been if I hadn't been this sort; I want to go and live out his potentialities, too. I haven't forgotten that there are birds in the bushes."

Bartley stopped and sat frowning into the fire, his shoulders thrust forward as if he were about to spring at something. Wilson watched him, wondering. His old pupil always stimulated him at first, and then vastly wearied him. The machinery was always pounding away in this man, and Wilson preferred companions of a more reflective habit of mind. He could not help feeling that there were unreasoning and unreasonable activities going on in Alexander all the while; that even after dinner, when most men achieve a decent impersonality, Bartley had merely closed the door of the engine-room and come up for an airing. The machinery itself was still pounding on.

Bartley's abstraction and Wilson's reflections were cut short by a rustle at the door, and almost before they could rise Mrs. Alexander was standing by the hearth. Alexander brought a chair for her, but she shook her head.

"No, dear, thank you. I only came in to see whether you and Professor Wilson were quite comfortable. I am going down to the music-room."

"Why not practice here? Wilson and I are growing very dull. We are tired of talk."

"Yes, I beg you, Mrs. Alexander," Wilson began, but he got no further.

"Why, certainly, if you won't find me too noisy. I am working on the Schumann `Carnival,' and, though I don't practice a great many hours, I am very methodical," Mrs. Alexander explained, as she crossed to an upright piano that stood at the back of the room, near the windows.

Wilson followed, and, having seen her seated, dropped into a chair behind her. She played brilliantly and with great musical feeling. Wilson could not imagine her permitting herself to do anything badly, but he was surprised at the cleanness of her execution. He wondered how a woman with so many duties had managed to keep herself up to a standard really professional. It must take a great deal of time, certainly, and Bartley must take a great deal of time. Wilson reflected that he had never before known a woman who had been able, for any considerable while, to support both a personal and an intellectual passion. Sitting behind her, he watched her with perplexed admiration, shading his eyes with his hand. In her dinner dress she looked even younger than in street clothes, and, for all her composure and self-sufficiency, she seemed to him strangely alert and vibrating, as if in her, too, there were something never altogether at rest. He felt that he knew pretty much what she demanded in people and what she demanded from life, and he wondered how she squared Bartley. After ten years she must know him; and however one took him, however much one admired him, one had to admit that he simply wouldn't square.

He was a natural force, certainly, but beyond that, Wilson felt, he was not anything very really or for very long at a time.

Wilson glanced toward the fire, where Bartley's profile was still wreathed in cigar smoke that curled up more and more slowly. His shoulders were sunk deep in the cushions and one hand hung large and passive over the arm of his chair. He had slipped on a purple velvet smoking-coat. His wife, Wilson surmised, had chosen it. She was clearly very proud of his good looks and his fine color. But, with the glow of an immediate interest gone out of it, the engineer's face looked tired, even a little haggard. The three lines in his forehead, directly above the nose, deepened as he sat thinking, and his powerful head drooped forward heavily. Although Alexander was only forty-three, Wilson thought that beneath his vigorous color he detected the dulling weariness of on-coming middle age.

The next afternoon, at the hour when the river was beginning to redden under the declining sun, Wilson again found himself facing Mrs. Alexander at the tea-table in the library.

"Well," he remarked, when he was bidden to give an account of himself, "there was a long morning with the psychologists, luncheon with Bartley at his club, more psychologists, and here I am. I've looked forward to this hour all day."

Mrs. Alexander smiled at him across the vapor from the kettle. "And do you remember where we stopped yesterday?"

"Perfectly. I was going to show you a picture. But I doubt whether I have color enough in me. Bartley makes me feel a faded monochrome. You can't get at the young Bartley except by means of color." Wilson paused and deliberated. Suddenly he broke out: "He wasn't a remarkable student, you know, though he was always strong in higher mathematics. His work in my own department was quite ordinary. It was as a powerfully equipped nature that I found him interesting. That is the most interesting thing a teacher can find. It has the fascination of a scientific discovery. We come across other pleasing and endearing qualities so much oftener than we find force."

"And, after all," said Mrs. Alexander, "that is the thing we all live upon. It is the thing that takes us forward."

Wilson thought she spoke a little wistfully. "Exactly," he assented warmly. "It builds the bridges into the future, over which the feet of every one of us will go."

"How interested I am to hear you put it in that way. The bridges into the future--I often say that to myself. Bartley's bridges always seem to me like that. Have you ever seen his first suspension bridge in Canada, the one he was doing when I first knew him? I hope you will see it sometime. We were married as soon as it was finished, and you will laugh when I tell you that it always has a rather bridal look to me. It is over the wildest river, with mists and clouds always battling about it, and it is as delicate as a cobweb hanging in the sky. It really was a bridge into the future. You have only to look at it to feel that it meant the beginning of a great career. But I have a photograph of it here." She drew a portfolio from behind a bookcase. "And there, you see, on the hill, is my aunt's house."

Wilson took up the photograph. "Bartley was telling me something about your aunt last night. She must have been a delightful person."

Winifred laughed. "The bridge, you see, was just at the foot of the hill, and the noise of the engines annoyed her very much at first. But after she met Bartley she pretended to like it, and said it was a good thing to be reminded that there were things going on in the world. She loved life, and Bartley brought a great deal of it in to her when he came to the house. Aunt Eleanor was very worldly in a frank, Early-Victorian manner. She liked men of action, and disliked young men who were careful of themselves and who, as she put it, were always trimming their wick as if they were afraid of their oil's giving out. MacKeller, Bartley's first chief, was an old friend of my aunt, and he told her that Bartley was a wild, ill-governed youth, which really pleased her very much. I remember we were sitting alone in the dusk after Bartley had been there for the first time. I knew that Aunt Eleanor had found him much to her taste, but she hadn't said anything. Presently she came out, with a chuckle: `MacKeller found him sowing wild oats in London, I believe. I hope he didn't stop him too soon. Life coquets with dashing fellows. The coming men are always like that. We must have him to dinner, my dear.' And we did. She grew much fonder of Bartley than she was of me. I had been studying in Vienna, and she thought that absurd. She was interested in the army and in politics, and she had a great contempt for music and art and philosophy. She used to declare that the Prince Consort had brought all that stuff over out of Germany. She always sniffed when Bartley asked me to play for him. She considered that a newfangled way of making a match of it."

When Alexander came in a few moments later, he found Wilson and his wife still confronting the photograph. "Oh, let us get that out of the way," he said, laughing. "Winifred, Thomas can bring my trunk down. I've decided to go over to New York to-morrow night and take a fast boat. I shall save two days."

CHAPTER II

On the night of his arrival in London, Alexander went immediately to the hotel on the Embankment at which he always stopped, and in the lobby he was accosted by an old acquaintance, Maurice Mainhall, who fell upon him with effusive cordiality and indicated a willingness to dine with him. Bartley never dined alone if he could help it, and Mainhall was a good gossip who always knew what had been going on in town; especially, he knew everything that was not printed in the newspapers. The nephew of one of the standard Victorian novelists, Mainhall bobbed about among the various literary cliques of London and its outlying suburbs, careful to lose touch with none of them. He had written a number of books himself; among them a "History of Dancing," a "History of Costume," a "Key to Shakespeare's Sonnets," a study of "The Poetry of Ernest Dowson," etc. Although Mainhall's enthusiasm was often tiresome, and although he was often unable to distinguish between facts and vivid figments of his imagination, his imperturbable good nature overcame even the people whom he bored most, so that they ended by becoming, in a reluctant manner, his friends. In appearance, Mainhall was astonishingly like the conventional stage-Englishman of American drama: tall and thin, with high, hitching shoulders and a small head glistening with closely brushed yellow hair. He spoke with an extreme Oxford accent, and when he was talking well, his face sometimes wore the rapt expression of a very emotional man listening to music. Mainhall liked Alexander because he was an engineer. He had preconceived ideas about everything, and his idea about Americans was that they should be engineers or mechanics. He hated them when they presumed to be anything else.

While they sat at dinner Mainhall acquainted Bartley with the fortunes of his old friends in London, and as they left the table he proposed that they should go to see Hugh MacConnell's new comedy, "Bog Lights."

"It's really quite the best thing MacConnell's done," he explained as they got into a hansom. "It's tremendously well put on, too. Florence Merrill and Cyril Henderson. But Hilda Burgoyne's the hit of the piece. Hugh's written a delightful part for her, and she's quite inexpressible. It's been on only two weeks, and I've been half a dozen times already. I happen to have MacConnell's box for tonight or there'd be no chance of our getting places. There's everything in seeing Hilda while she's fresh in a part. She's apt to grow a bit stale after a time. The ones who have any imagination do."

"Hilda Burgoyne!" Alexander exclaimed mildly. "Why, I haven't heard of her for--years."

Mainhall laughed. "Then you can't have heard much at all, my dear Alexander. It's only lately, since MacConnell and his set have got hold of her, that she's come up. Myself, I always knew she had it in her. If we had one real critic in London--but what can one expect? Do you know, Alexander,"--Mainhall looked with perplexity up into the top of the hansom and rubbed his pink cheek with his gloved finger,-- "do you know, I sometimes think of taking to criticism seriously myself. In a way, it would be a sacrifice; but, dear me, we do need some one."

Just then they drove up to the Duke of York's, so Alexander did not commit himself, but followed Mainhall into the theatre. When they entered the stage-box on the left the first act was well under way, the scene being the interior of a cabin in the south of Ireland. As they sat down, a burst of applause drew Alexander's attention to the stage. Miss Burgoyne and her donkey were thrusting their heads in at the half door. "After all," he reflected, "there's small probability of her recognizing me. She doubtless hasn't thought of me for years." He felt the enthusiasm of the house at once, and in a few moments he was caught up by the current of MacConnell's irresistible comedy. The audience had come forewarned, evidently, and whenever the ragged slip of a donkey-girl ran upon the stage there was a deep murmur of approbation, every one smiled and glowed, and Mainhall hitched his heavy chair a little nearer the brass railing.

"You see," he murmured in Alexander's ear, as the curtain fell on the first act, "one almost never sees a part like that done without smartness or mawkishness. Of course, Hilda is Irish,--the Burgoynes have been stage people for generations,--and she has the Irish voice. It's delightful to hear it in a London theatre. That laugh, now, when she doubles over at the hips--who ever heard it out of Galway? She saves her hand, too. She's at her best in the second act. She's really MacConnell's poetic motif, you see; makes the whole thing a fairy tale."

The second act opened before Philly Doyle's underground still, with Peggy and her battered donkey come in to smuggle a load of potheen across the bog, and to bring Philly word of what was doing in the world without, and of what was happening along the roadsides and ditches with the first gleam of fine weather. Alexander, annoyed by Mainhall's sighs and exclamations, watched her with keen, half-skeptical interest. As Mainhall had said, she was the second act; the plot and feeling alike depended upon her lightness of foot, her lightness of touch, upon the shrewdness and deft fancifulness that played alternately, and sometimes together, in her mirthful brown eyes. When she began to dance, by way of showing the gossoons what she had seen in the fairy rings at night, the house broke into a prolonged uproar. After her dance she withdrew from the dialogue and retreated to the ditch wall back of Philly's burrow, where she sat singing "The Rising of the Moon" and making a wreath of primroses for her donkey.

When the act was over Alexander and Mainhall strolled out into the corridor. They met a good many acquaintances; Mainhall, indeed, knew almost every one, and he babbled on incontinently, screwing his small head about over his high collar. Presently he hailed a tall, bearded man, grim-browed and rather battered-looking, who had his opera cloak on his arm and his hat in his hand, and who seemed to be on the point of leaving the theatre.

"MacConnell, let me introduce Mr. Bartley Alexander. I say! It's going famously to-night, Mac. And what an audience! You'll never do anything like this again, mark me. A man writes to the top of his bent only once."

The playwright gave Mainhall a curious look out of his deep-set faded eyes and made a wry face. "And have I done anything so fool as that, now?" he asked.

"That's what I was saying," Mainhall lounged a little nearer and dropped into a tone even more conspicuously confidential. "And you'll never bring Hilda out like this again. Dear me, Mac, the girl couldn't possibly be better, you know."

MacConnell grunted. "She'll do well enough if she keeps her pace and doesn't go off on us in the middle of the season, as she's more than like to do."

He nodded curtly and made for the door, dodging acquaintances as he went.

"Poor old Hugh," Mainhall murmured. "He's hit terribly hard. He's been wanting to marry Hilda these three years and more. She doesn't take up with anybody, you know. Irene Burgoyne, one of her family, told me in confidence that there was a romance somewhere back in the beginning. One of your countrymen, Alexander, by the way; an American student whom she met in Paris, I believe. I dare say it's quite true that there's never been any one else." Mainhall vouched for her constancy with a loftiness that made Alexander smile, even while a kind of rapid excitement was tingling through him. Blinking up at the lights, Mainhall added in his luxurious, worldly way: "She's an elegant little person, and quite capable of an extravagant bit of sentiment like that. Here comes Sir Harry Towne. He's another who's awfully keen about her. Let me introduce you. Sir Harry Towne, Mr. Bartley Alexander, the American engineer."

Sir Harry Towne bowed and said that he had met Mr. Alexander and his wife in Tokyo.

Mainhall cut in impatiently.

"I say, Sir Harry, the little girl's going famously to-night, isn't she?"

Sir Harry wrinkled his brows judiciously. "Do you know, I thought the dance a bit conscious to-night, for the first time. The fact is, she's feeling rather seedy, poor child. Westmere and I were back after the first act, and we thought she seemed quite uncertain of herself. A little attack of nerves, possibly."

He bowed as the warning bell rang, and Mainhall whispered: "You know Lord Westmere, of course,--the stooped man with the long gray mustache, talking to Lady Dowle. Lady Westmere is very fond of Hilda."

When they reached their box the house was darkened and the orchestra was playing "The Cloak of Old Gaul." In a moment Peggy was on the stage again, and Alexander applauded vigorously with the rest. He even leaned forward over the rail a little. For some reason he felt pleased and flattered by the enthusiasm of the audience. In the half-light he looked about at the stalls and boxes and smiled a little consciously, recalling with amusement Sir Harry's judicial frown. He was beginning to feel a keen interest in the slender, barefoot donkey-girl who slipped in and out of the play, singing, like some one winding through a hilly field. He leaned forward and beamed felicitations as warmly as Mainhall himself when, at the end of the play, she came again and again before the curtain, panting a little and flushed, her eyes dancing and her eager, nervous little mouth tremulous with excitement.

When Alexander returned to his hotel--he shook Mainhall at the door of the theatre--he had some supper brought up to his room, and it was late before he went to bed. He had not thought of Hilda Burgoyne for years; indeed, he had almost forgotten her. He had last written to her from Canada, after he first met Winifred, telling her that everything was changed with him--that he had met a woman whom he would marry if he could; if he could not, then all the more was everything changed for him. Hilda had never replied to his letter. He felt guilty and unhappy about her for a time, but after Winifred promised to marry him he really forgot Hilda altogether. When he wrote her that everything was changed for him, he was telling the truth. After he met Winifred Pemberton he seemed to himself like a different man. One night when he and Winifred were sitting together on the bridge, he told her that things had happened while he was studying abroad that he was sorry for,--one thing in particular,--and he asked her whether she thought she ought to know about them. She considered a moment and then said "No, I think not, though I am glad you ask me. You see, one can't be jealous about things in general; but about particular, definite, personal things,"--here she had thrown her hands up to his shoulders with a quick, impulsive gesture--"oh, about those I should be very jealous. I should torture myself--I couldn't help it." After that it was easy to forget, actually to forget. He wondered to-night, as he poured his wine, how many times he had thought of Hilda in the last ten years. He had been in London more or less, but he had never happened to hear of her. "All the same," he lifted his glass, "here's to you, little Hilda. You've made things come your way, and I never thought you'd do it.

"Of course," he reflected, "she always had that combination of something homely and sensible, and something utterly wild and daft. But I never thought she'd do anything. She hadn't much ambition then, and she was too fond of trifles. She must care about the theatre a great deal more than she used to. Perhaps she has me to thank for something, after all. Sometimes a little jolt like that does one good. She was a daft, generous little thing. I'm glad she's held her own since. After all, we were awfully young. It was youth and poverty and proximity, and everything was young and kindly. I shouldn't wonder if she could laugh about it with me now. I shouldn't wonder-- But they've probably spoiled her, so that she'd be tiresome if one met her again."

Bartley smiled and yawned and went to bed.

CHAPTER III

The next evening Alexander dined alone at a club, and at about nine o'clock he dropped in at the Duke of York's. The house was sold out and he stood through the second act. When he returned to his hotel he examined the new directory, and found Miss Burgoyne's address still given as off Bedford Square, though at a new number. He remembered that, in so far as she had been brought up at all, she had been brought up in Bloomsbury. Her father and mother played in the provinces most of the year, and she was left a great deal in the care of an old aunt who was crippled by rheumatism and who had had to leave the stage altogether. In the days when Alexander knew her, Hilda always managed to have a lodging of some sort about Bedford Square, because she clung tenaciously to such scraps and shreds of memories as were connected with it. The mummy room of the British Museum had been one of the chief delights of her childhood. That forbidding pile was the goal of her truant fancy, and she was sometimes taken there for a treat, as other children are taken to the theatre. It was long since Alexander had thought of any of these things, but now they came back to him quite fresh, and had a significance they did not have when they were first told him in his restless twenties. So she was still in the old neighborhood, near Bedford Square. The new number probably meant increased prosperity. He hoped so. He would like to know that she was snugly settled. He looked at his watch. It was a quarter past ten; she would not be home for a good two hours yet, and he might as well walk over and have a look at the place. He remembered the shortest way.

It was a warm, smoky evening, and there was a grimy moon. He went through Covent Garden to Oxford Street, and as he turned into Museum Street he walked more slowly, smiling at his own nervousness as he approached the sullen gray mass at the end. He had not been inside the Museum, actually, since he and Hilda used to meet there; sometimes to set out for gay adventures at Twickenham or Richmond, sometimes to linger about the place for a while and to ponder by Lord Elgin's marbles upon the lastingness of some things, or, in the mummy room, upon the awful brevity of others. Since then Bartley had always thought of the British Museum as the ultimate repository of mortality, where all the dead things in the world were assembled to make one's hour of youth the more precious. One trembled lest before he got out it might somehow escape him, lest he might drop the glass from over-eagerness and see it shivered on the stone floor at his feet. How one hid his youth under his coat and hugged it! And how good it was to turn one's back upon all that vaulted cold, to take Hilda's arm and hurry out of the great door and down the steps into the sunlight among the pigeons--to know that the warm and vital thing within him was still there and had not been snatched away to flush Caesar's lean cheek or to feed the veins of some bearded Assyrian king. They in their day had carried the flaming liquor, but to-day was his! So the song used to run in his head those summer mornings a dozen years ago. Alexander walked by the place very quietly, as if he were afraid of waking some one.

He crossed Bedford Square and found the number he was looking for. The house, a comfortable, well-kept place enough, was dark except for the four front windows on the second floor, where a low, even light was burning behind the white muslin sash curtains. Outside there were window boxes, painted white and full of flowers. Bartley was making a third round of the Square when he heard the far-flung hoof-beats of a hansom-cab horse, driven rapidly. He looked at his watch, and was astonished to find that it was a few minutes after twelve. He turned and walked back along the iron railing as the cab came up to Hilda's number and stopped. The hansom must have been one that she employed regularly, for she did not stop to pay the driver. She stepped out quickly and lightly. He heard her cheerful "Good-night, cabby," as she ran up the steps and opened the door with a latchkey. In a few moments the lights flared up brightly behind the white curtains, and as he walked away he heard a window raised. But he had gone too far to look up without turning round. He went back to his hotel, feeling that he had had a good evening, and he slept well.

For the next few days Alexander was very busy. He took a desk in the office of a Scotch engineering firm on Henrietta Street, and was at work almost constantly.

He avoided the clubs and usually dined alone at his hotel. One afternoon, after he had tea, he started for a walk down the Embankment toward Westminster, intending to end his stroll at Bedford Square and to ask whether Miss Burgoyne would let him take her to the theatre. But he did not go so far. When he reached the Abbey, he turned back and crossed Westminster Bridge and sat down to watch the trails of smoke behind the Houses of Parliament catch fire with the sunset. The slender towers were washed by a rain of golden light and licked by little flickering flames; Somerset House and the bleached gray pinnacles about Whitehall were floated in a luminous haze. The yellow light poured through the trees and the leaves seemed to burn with soft fires. There was a smell of acacias in the air everywhere, and the laburnums were dripping gold over the walls of the gardens. It was a sweet, lonely kind of summer evening. Remembering Hilda as she used to be, was doubtless more satisfactory than seeing her as she must be now--and, after all, Alexander asked himself, what was it but his own young years that he was remembering?

He crossed back to Westminster, went up to the Temple, and sat down to smoke in the Middle Temple gardens, listening to the thin voice of the fountain and smelling the spice of the sycamores that came out heavily in the damp evening air. He thought, as he sat there, about a great many things: about his own youth and Hilda's; above all, he thought of how glorious it had been, and how quickly it had passed; and, when it had passed, how little worth while anything was. None of the things he had gained in the least compensated. In the last six years his reputation had become, as the saying is, popular. Four years ago he had been called to Japan to deliver, at the Emperor's request, a course of lectures at the Imperial University, and had instituted reforms throughout the islands, not only in the practice of bridge-building but in drainage and road-making. On his return he had undertaken the bridge at Moorlock, in Canada, the most important piece of bridge-building going on in the world,--a test, indeed, of how far the latest practice in bridge structure could be carried. It was a spectacular undertaking by reason of its very size, and Bartley realized that, whatever else he might do, he would probably always be known as the engineer who designed the great Moorlock Bridge, the longest cantilever in existence. Yet it was to him the least satisfactory thing he had ever done. He was cramped in every way by a niggardly commission, and was using lighter structural material than he thought proper. He had vexations enough, too, with his work at home. He had several bridges under way in the United States, and they were always being held up by strikes and delays resulting from a general industrial unrest.

Though Alexander often told himself he had never put more into his work than he had done in the last few years, he had to admit that he had never got so little out of it. He was paying for success, too, in the demands made on his time by boards of civic enterprise and committees of public welfare. The obligations imposed by his wife's fortune and position were sometimes distracting to a man who followed his profession, and he was expected to be interested in a great many worthy endeavors on her account as well as on his own. His existence was becoming a network of great and little details. He had expected that success would bring him freedom and power; but it had brought only power that was in itself another kind of restraint. He had always meant to keep his personal liberty at all costs, as old MacKeller, his first chief, had done, and not, like so many American engineers, to become a part of a professional movement, a cautious board member, a Nestor de pontibus. He happened to be engaged in work of public utility, but he was not willing to become what is called a public man. He found himself living exactly the kind of life he had determined to escape. What, he asked himself, did he want with these genial honors and substantial comforts? Hardships and difficulties he had carried lightly; overwork had not exhausted him; but this dead calm of middle life which confronted him,--of that he was afraid. He was not ready for it. It was like being buried alive. In his youth he would not have believed such a thing possible. The one thing he had really wanted all his life was to be free; and there was still something unconquered in him, something besides the strong work-horse that his profession had made of him. He felt rich to-night in the possession of that unstultified survival; in the light of his experience, it was more precious than honors or achievement. In all those busy, successful years there had been nothing so good as this hour of wild light-heartedness. This feeling was the only happiness that was real to him, and such hours were the only ones in which he could feel his own continuous identity--feel the boy he had been in the rough days of the old West, feel the youth who had worked his way across the ocean on a cattle-ship and gone to study in Paris without a dollar in his pocket. The man who sat in his offices in Boston was only a powerful machine. Under the activities of that machine the person who, in such moments as this, he felt to be himself, was fading and dying. He remembered how, when he was a little boy and his father called him in the morning, he used to leap from his bed into the full consciousness of himself. That consciousness was Life itself. Whatever took its place, action, reflection, the power of concentrated thought, were only functions of a mechanism useful to society; things that could be bought in the market. There was only one thing that had an absolute value for each individual, and it was just that original impulse, that internal heat, that feeling of one's self in one's own breast.

When Alexander walked back to his hotel, the red and green lights were blinking along the docks on the farther shore, and the soft white stars were shining in the wide sky above the river.

The next night, and the next, Alexander repeated this same foolish performance. It was always Miss Burgoyne whom he started out to find, and he got no farther than the Temple gardens and the Embankment. It was a pleasant kind of loneliness. To a man who was so little given to reflection, whose dreams always took the form of definite ideas, reaching into the future, there was a seductive excitement in renewing old experiences in imagination. He started out upon these walks half guiltily, with a curious longing and expectancy which were wholly gratified by solitude. Solitude, but not solitariness; for he walked shoulder to shoulder with a shadowy companion--not little Hilda Burgoyne, by any means, but some one vastly dearer to him than she had ever been--his own young self, the youth who had waited for him upon the steps of the British Museum that night, and who, though he had tried to pass so quietly, had known him and come down and linked an arm in his.

It was not until long afterward that Alexander learned that for him this youth was the most dangerous of companions.

One Sunday evening, at Lady Walford's, Alexander did at last meet Hilda Burgoyne. Mainhall had told him that she would probably be there. He looked about for her rather nervously, and finally found her at the farther end of the large drawing-room, the centre of a circle of men, young and old. She was apparently telling them a story. They were all laughing and bending toward her. When she saw Alexander, she rose quickly and put out her hand. The other men drew back a little to let him approach.

"Mr. Alexander! I am delighted. Have you been in London long?"

Bartley bowed, somewhat laboriously, over her hand. "Long enough to have seen you more than once. How fine it all is!"

She laughed as if she were pleased. "I'm glad you think so. I like it. Won't you join us here?"

"Miss Burgoyne was just telling us about a donkey-boy she had in Galway last summer," Sir Harry Towne explained as the circle closed up again. Lord Westmere stroked his long white mustache with his bloodless hand and looked at Alexander blankly. Hilda was a good story-teller. She was sitting on the edge of her chair, as if she had alighted there for a moment only. Her primrose satin gown seemed like a soft sheath for her slender, supple figure, and its delicate color suited her white Irish skin and brown hair. Whatever she wore, people felt the charm of her active, girlish body with its slender hips and quick, eager shoulders. Alexander heard little of the story, but he watched Hilda intently. She must certainly, he reflected, be thirty, and he was honestly delighted to see that the years had treated her so indulgently. If her face had changed at all, it was in a slight hardening of the mouth--still eager enough to be very disconcerting at times, he felt--and in an added air of self-possession and self-reliance. She carried her head, too, a little more resolutely.

When the story was finished, Miss Burgoyne turned pointedly to Alexander, and the other men drifted away.

"I thought I saw you in MacConnell's box with Mainhall one evening, but I supposed you had left town before this."

She looked at him frankly and cordially, as if he were indeed merely an old friend whom she was glad to meet again.

"No, I've been mooning about here."

Hilda laughed gayly. "Mooning! I see you mooning! You must be the busiest man in the world. Time and success have done well by you, you know. You're handsomer than ever and you've gained a grand manner."

Alexander blushed and bowed. "Time and success have been good friends to both of us. Aren't you tremendously pleased with yourself?"

She laughed again and shrugged her shoulders. "Oh, so-so. But I want to hear about you. Several years ago I read such a lot in the papers about the wonderful things you did in Japan, and how the Emperor decorated you. What was it, Commander of the Order of the Rising Sun? That sounds like `The Mikado.' And what about your new bridge--in Canada, isn't it, and it's to be the longest one in the world and has some queer name I can't remember."

Bartley shook his head and smiled drolly. "Since when have you been interested in bridges? Or have you learned to be interested in everything? And is that a part of success?"

"Why, how absurd! As if I were not always interested!" Hilda exclaimed.

"Well, I think we won't talk about bridges here, at any rate." Bartley looked down at the toe of her yellow slipper which was tapping the rug impatiently under the hem of her gown. "But I wonder whether you'd think me impertinent if I asked you to let me come to see you sometime and tell you about them?"

"Why should I? Ever so many people come on Sunday afternoons."

"I know. Mainhall offered to take me. But you must know that I've been in London several times within the last few years, and you might very well think that just now is a rather inopportune time--"

She cut him short. "Nonsense. One of the pleasantest things about success is that it makes people want to look one up, if that's what you mean. I'm like every one else--more agreeable to meet when things are going well with me. Don't you suppose it gives me any pleasure to do something that people like?"

"Does it? Oh, how fine it all is, your coming on like this! But I didn't want you to think it was because of that I wanted to see you." He spoke very seriously and looked down at the floor.

Hilda studied him in wide-eyed astonishment for a moment, and then broke into a low, amused laugh. "My dear Mr. Alexander, you have strange delicacies. If you please, that is exactly why you wish to see me. We understand that, do we not?"

Bartley looked ruffled and turned the seal ring on his little finger about awkwardly.

Hilda leaned back in her chair, watching him indulgently out of her shrewd eyes. "Come, don't be angry, but don't try to pose for me, or to be anything but what you are. If you care to come, it's yourself I'll be glad to see, and you thinking well of yourself. Don't try to wear a cloak of humility; it doesn't become you. Stalk in as you are and don't make excuses. I'm not accustomed to inquiring into the motives of my guests. That would hardly be safe, even for Lady Walford, in a great house like this."

"Sunday afternoon, then," said Alexander, as she rose to join her hostess. "How early may I come?"

She gave him her hand and flushed and laughed. He bent over it a little stiffly. She went away on Lady Walford's arm, and as he stood watching her yellow train glide down the long floor he looked rather sullen. He felt that he had not come out of it very brilliantly.

CHAPTER IV

On Sunday afternoon Alexander remembered Miss Burgoyne's invitation and called at her apartment. He found it a delightful little place and he met charming people there. Hilda lived alone, attended by a very pretty and competent French servant who answered the door and brought in the tea. Alexander arrived early, and some twenty-odd people dropped in during the course of the afternoon. Hugh MacConnell came with his sister, and stood about, managing his tea-cup awkwardly and watching every one out of his deepset, faded eyes. He seemed to have made a resolute effort at tidiness of attire, and his sister, a robust, florid woman with a splendid joviality about her, kept eyeing his freshly creased clothes apprehensively. It was not very long, indeed, before his coat hung with a discouraged sag from his gaunt shoulders and his hair and beard were rumpled as if he had been out in a gale. His dry humor went under a cloud of absent-minded kindliness which, Mainhall explained, always overtook him here. He was never so witty or so sharp here as elsewhere, and Alexander thought he behaved as if he were an elderly relative come in to a young girl's party.

The editor of a monthly review came with his wife, and Lady Kildare, the Irish philanthropist, brought her young nephew, Robert Owen, who had come up from Oxford, and who was visibly excited and gratified by his first introduction to Miss Burgoyne. Hilda was very nice to him, and he sat on the edge of his chair, flushed with his conversational efforts and moving his chin about nervously over his high collar. Sarah Frost, the novelist, came with her husband, a very genial and placid old scholar who had become slightly deranged upon the subject of the fourth dimension. On other matters he was perfectly rational and he was easy and pleasing in conversation. He looked very much like Agassiz, and his wife, in her old-fashioned black silk dress, overskirted and tight-sleeved, reminded Alexander of the early pictures of Mrs. Browning. Hilda seemed particularly fond of this quaint couple, and Bartley himself was so pleased with their mild and thoughtful converse that he took his leave when they did, and walked with them over to Oxford Street, where they waited for their 'bus. They asked him to come to see them in Chelsea, and they spoke very tenderly of Hilda. "She's a dear, unworldly little thing," said the philosopher absently; "more like the stage people of my young days--folk of simple manners. There aren't many such left. American tours have spoiled them, I'm afraid. They have all grown very smart. Lamb wouldn't care a great deal about many of them, I fancy."

Alexander went back to Bedford Square a second Sunday afternoon. He had a long talk with MacConnell, but he got no word with Hilda alone, and he left in a discontented state of mind. For the rest of the week he was nervous and unsettled, and kept rushing his work as if he were preparing for immediate departure. On Thursday afternoon he cut short a committee meeting, jumped into a hansom, and drove to Bedford Square. He sent up his card, but it came back to him with a message scribbled across the front.

So sorry I can't see you. Will you come and
  dine with me Sunday evening at half-past seven?

H.B.

When Bartley arrived at Bedford Square on Sunday evening, Marie, the pretty little French girl, met him at the door and conducted him upstairs. Hilda was writing in her living-room, under the light of a tall desk lamp. Bartley recognized the primrose satin gown she had worn that first evening at Lady Walford's.

"I'm so pleased that you think me worth that yellow dress, you know," he said, taking her hand and looking her over admiringly from the toes of her canary slippers to her smoothly parted brown hair. "Yes, it's very, very pretty. Every one at Lady Walford's was looking at it."

Hilda curtsied. "Is that why you think it pretty? I've no need for fine clothes in Mac's play this time, so I can afford a few duddies for myself. It's owing to that same chance, by the way, that I am able to ask you to dinner. I don't need Marie to dress me this season, so she keeps house for me, and my little Galway girl has gone home for a visit. I should never have asked you if Molly had been here, for I remember you don't like English cookery."

Alexander walked about the room, looking at everything.

"I haven't had a chance yet to tell you what a jolly little place I think this is. Where did you get those etchings? They're quite unusual, aren't they?"

"Lady Westmere sent them to me from Rome last Christmas. She is very much interested in the American artist who did them. They are all sketches made about the Villa d'Este, you see. He painted that group of cypresses for the Salon, and it was bought for the Luxembourg."

Alexander walked over to the bookcases. "It's the air of the whole place here that I like. You haven't got anything that doesn't belong. Seems to me it looks particularly well to-night. And you have so many flowers. I like these little yellow irises."

"Rooms always look better by lamplight--in London, at least. Though Marie is clean--really clean, as the French are. Why do you look at the flowers so critically? Marie got them all fresh in Covent Garden market yesterday morning."

"I'm glad," said Alexander simply. "I can't tell you how glad I am to have you so pretty and comfortable here, and to hear every one saying such nice things about you. You've got awfully nice friends," he added humbly, picking up a little jade elephant from her desk. "Those fellows are all very loyal, even Mainhall. They don't talk of any one else as they do of you."

Hilda sat down on the couch and said seriously: "I've a neat little sum in the bank, too, now, and I own a mite of a hut in Galway. It's not worth much, but I love it. I've managed to save something every year, and that with helping my three sisters now and then, and tiding poor Cousin Mike over bad seasons. He's that gifted, you know, but he will drink and loses more good engagements than other fellows ever get. And I've traveled a bit, too."

Marie opened the door and smilingly announced that dinner was served.

"My dining-room," Hilda explained, as she led the way, "is the tiniest place you have ever seen."

It was a tiny room, hung all round with French prints, above which ran a shelf full of china. Hilda saw Alexander look up at it.

"It's not particularly rare," she said, "but some of it was my mother's. Heaven knows how she managed to keep it whole, through all our wanderings, or in what baskets and bundles and theatre trunks it hasn't been stowed away. We always had our tea out of those blue cups when I was a little girl, sometimes in the queerest lodgings, and sometimes on a trunk at the theatre--queer theatres, for that matter."

It was a wonderful little dinner. There was watercress soup, and sole, and a delightful omelette stuffed with mushrooms and truffles, and two small rare ducklings, and artichokes, and a dry yellow Rhone wine of which Bartley had always been very fond. He drank it appreciatively and remarked that there was still no other he liked so well.

"I have some champagne for you, too. I don't drink it myself, but I like to see it behave when it's poured. There is nothing else that looks so jolly."

"Thank you. But I don't like it so well as this." Bartley held the yellow wine against the light and squinted into it as he turned the glass slowly about. "You have traveled, you say. Have you been in Paris much these late years?"

Hilda lowered one of the candle-shades carefully. "Oh, yes, I go over to Paris often. There are few changes in the old Quarter. Dear old Madame Anger is dead--but perhaps you don't remember her?"

"Don't I, though! I'm so sorry to hear it. How did her son turn out? I remember how she saved and scraped for him, and how he always lay abed till ten o'clock. He was the laziest fellow at the Beaux Arts; and that's saying a good deal."

"Well, he is still clever and lazy. They say he is a good architect when he will work. He's a big, handsome creature, and he hates Americans as much as ever. But Angel--do you remember Angel?"

"Perfectly. Did she ever get back to Brittany and her bains de mer?"

"Ah, no. Poor Angel! She got tired of cooking and scouring the coppers in Madame Anger's little kitchen, so she ran away with a soldier, and then with another soldier. Too bad! She still lives about the Quarter, and, though there is always a soldat, she has become a blanchisseuse de fin. She did my blouses beautifully the last time I was there, and was so delighted to see me again. I gave her all my old clothes, even my old hats, though she always wears her Breton headdress. Her hair is still like flax, and her blue eyes are just like a baby's, and she has the same three freckles on her little nose, and talks about going back to her bains de mer."

Bartley looked at Hilda across the yellow light of the candles and broke into a low, happy laugh. "How jolly it was being young, Hilda! Do you remember that first walk we took together in Paris? We walked down to the Place Saint-Michel to buy some lilacs. Do you remember how sweet they smelled?"

"Indeed I do. Come, we'll have our coffee in the other room, and you can smoke."

Hilda rose quickly, as if she wished to change the drift of their talk, but Bartley found it pleasant to continue it.

"What a warm, soft spring evening that was," he went on, as they sat down in the study with the coffee on a little table between them; "and the sky, over the bridges, was just the color of the lilacs. We walked on down by the river, didn't we?"

Hilda laughed and looked at him questioningly. He saw a gleam in her eyes that he remembered even better than the episode he was recalling.

"I think we did," she answered demurely. "It was on the Quai we met that woman who was crying so bitterly. I gave her a spray of lilac, I remember, and you gave her a franc. I was frightened at your prodigality."

"I expect it was the last franc I had. What a strong brown face she had, and very tragic. She looked at us with such despair and longing, out from under her black shawl. What she wanted from us was neither our flowers nor our francs, but just our youth. I remember it touched me so. I would have given her some of mine off my back, if I could. I had enough and to spare then," Bartley mused, and looked thoughtfully at his cigar.

They were both remembering what the woman had said when she took the money: "God give you a happy love!" It was not in the ingratiating tone of the habitual beggar: it had come out of the depths of the poor creature's sorrow, vibrating with pity for their youth and despair at the terribleness of human life; it had the anguish of a voice of prophecy. Until she spoke, Bartley had not realized that he was in love. The strange woman, and her passionate sentence that rang out so sharply, had frightened them both. They went home sadly with the lilacs, back to the Rue Saint-Jacques, walking very slowly, arm in arm. When they reached the house where Hilda lodged, Bartley went across the court with her, and up the dark old stairs to the third landing; and there he had kissed her for the first time. He had shut his eyes to give him the courage, he remembered, and she had trembled so--

Bartley started when Hilda rang the little bell beside her. "Dear me, why did you do that? I had quite forgotten--I was back there. It was very jolly," he murmured lazily, as Marie came in to take away the coffee.

Hilda laughed and went over to the piano. "Well, we are neither of us twenty now, you know. Have I told you about my new play? Mac is writing one; really for me this time. You see, I'm coming on."

"I've seen nothing else. What kind of a part is it? Shall you wear yellow gowns? I hope so."

He was looking at her round slender figure, as she stood by the piano, turning over a pile of music, and he felt the energy in every line of it.

"No, it isn't a dress-up part. He doesn't seem to fancy me in fine feathers. He says I ought to be minding the pigs at home, and I suppose I ought. But he's given me some good Irish songs. Listen."

She sat down at the piano and sang. When she finished, Alexander shook himself out of a reverie.

"Sing `The Harp That Once,' Hilda. You used to sing it so well."

"Nonsense. Of course I can't really sing, except the way my mother and grandmother did before me. Most actresses nowadays learn to sing properly, so I tried a master; but he confused me, just!"

Alexander laughed. "All the same, sing it, Hilda."

Hilda started up from the stool and moved restlessly toward the window. "It's really too warm in this room to sing. Don't you feel it?"

Alexander went over and opened the window for her. "Aren't you afraid to let the wind low like that on your neck? Can't I get a scarf or something?"

"Ask a theatre lady if she's afraid of drafts!" Hilda laughed. "But perhaps, as I'm so warm--give me your handkerchief. There, just in front." He slipped the corners carefully under her shoulder-straps. "There, that will do. It looks like a bib." She pushed his hand away quickly and stood looking out into the deserted square. "Isn't London a tomb on Sunday night?"

Alexander caught the agitation in her voice. He stood a little behind her, and tried to steady himself as he said: "It's soft and misty. See how white the stars are."

For a long time neither Hilda nor Bartley spoke. They stood close together, looking out into the wan, watery sky, breathing always more quickly and lightly, and it seemed as if all the clocks in the world had stopped. Suddenly he moved the clenched hand he held behind him and dropped it violently at his side. He felt a tremor run through the slender yellow figure in front of him.

She caught his handkerchief from her throat and thrust it at him without turning round. "Here, take it. You must go now, Bartley. Good-night."

Bartley leaned over her shoulder, without touching her, and whispered in her ear: "You are giving me a chance?"

"Yes. Take it and go. This isn't fair, you know. Good-night."

Alexander unclenched the two hands at his sides. With one he threw down the window and with the other--still standing behind her--he drew her back against him.

She uttered a little cry, threw her arms over her head, and drew his face down to hers. "Are you going to let me love you a little, Bartley?" she whispered.

CHAPTER V

It was the afternoon of the day before Christmas. Mrs. Alexander had been driving about all the morning, leaving presents at the houses of her friends. She lunched alone, and as she rose from the table she spoke to the butler: "Thomas, I am going down to the kitchen now to see Norah. In half an hour you are to bring the greens up from the cellar and put them in the library. Mr. Alexander will be home at three to hang them himself. Don't forget the stepladder, and plenty of tacks and string. You may bring the azaleas upstairs. Take the white one to Mr. Alexander's study. Put the two pink ones in this room, and the red one in the drawing-room."

A little before three o'clock Mrs. Alexander went into the library to see that everything was ready. She pulled the window shades high, for the weather was dark and stormy, and there was little light, even in the streets. A foot of snow had fallen during the morning, and the wide space over the river was thick with flying flakes that fell and wreathed the masses of floating ice. Winifred was standing by the window when she heard the front door open. She hurried to the hall as Alexander came stamping in, covered with snow. He kissed her joyfully and brushed away the snow that fell on her hair.

"I wish I had asked you to meet me at the office and walk home with me, Winifred. The Common is beautiful. The boys have swept the snow off the pond and are skating furiously. Did the cyclamens come?"

"An hour ago. What splendid ones! But aren't you frightfully extravagant?"

"Not for Christmas-time. I'll go upstairs and change my coat. I shall be down in a moment. Tell Thomas to get everything ready."

When Alexander reappeared, he took his wife's arm and went with her into the library. "When did the azaleas get here? Thomas has got the white one in my room."

"I told him to put it there."

"But, I say, it's much the finest of the lot!"

"That's why I had it put there. There is too much color in that room for a red one, you know."

Bartley began to sort the greens. "It looks very splendid there, but I feel piggish to have it. However, we really spend more time there than anywhere else in the house. Will you hand me the holly?"

He climbed up the stepladder, which creaked under his weight, and began to twist the tough stems of the holly into the frame-work of the chandelier.

"I forgot to tell you that I had a letter from Wilson, this morning, explaining his telegram. He is coming on because an old uncle up in Vermont has conveniently died and left Wilson a little money--something like ten thousand. He's coming on to settle up the estate. Won't it be jolly to have him?"

"And how fine that he's come into a little money. I can see him posting down State Street to the steamship offices. He will get a good many trips out of that ten thousand. What can have detained him? I expected him here for luncheon."

"Those trains from Albany are always late. He'll be along sometime this afternoon. And now, don't you want to go upstairs and lie down for an hour? You've had a busy morning and I don't want you to be tired to-night."

After his wife went upstairs Alexander worked energetically at the greens for a few moments. Then, as he was cutting off a length of string, he sighed suddenly and sat down, staring out of the window at the snow. The animation died out of his face, but in his eyes there was a restless light, a look of apprehension and suspense. He kept clasping and unclasping his big hands as if he were trying to realize something. The clock ticked through the minutes of a half-hour and the afternoon outside began to thicken and darken turbidly. Alexander, since he first sat down, had not changed his position. He leaned forward, his hands between his knees, scarcely breathing, as if he were holding himself away from his surroundings, from the room, and from the very chair in which he sat, from everything except the wild eddies of snow above the river on which his eyes were fixed with feverish intentness, as if he were trying to project himself thither. When at last Lucius Wilson was announced, Alexander sprang eagerly to his feet and hurried to meet his old instructor.

"Hello, Wilson. What luck! Come into the library. We are to have a lot of people to dinner to-night, and Winifred's lying down. You will excuse her, won't you? And now what about yourself? Sit down and tell me everything."

"I think I'd rather move about, if you don't mind. I've been sitting in the train for a week, it seems to me." Wilson stood before the fire with his hands behind him and looked about the room. "You HAVE been busy. Bartley, if I'd had my choice of all possible places in which to spend Christmas, your house would certainly be the place I'd have chosen. Happy people do a great deal for their friends. A house like this throws its warmth out. I felt it distinctly as I was coming through the Berkshires. I could scarcely believe that I was to see Mrs. Bartley again so soon."

"Thank you, Wilson. She'll be as glad to see you. Shall we have tea now? I'll ring for Thomas to clear away this litter. Winifred says I always wreck the house when I try to do anything. Do you know, I am quite tired. Looks as if I were not used to work, doesn't it?" Alexander laughed and dropped into a chair. "You know, I'm sailing the day after New Year's."

"Again? Why, you've been over twice since I was here in the spring, haven't you?"

"Oh, I was in London about ten days in the summer. Went to escape the hot weather more than anything else. I shan't be gone more than a month this time. Winifred and I have been up in Canada for most of the autumn. That Moorlock Bridge is on my back all the time. I never had so much trouble with a job before." Alexander moved about restlessly and fell to poking the fire.

"Haven't I seen in the papers that there is some trouble about a tidewater bridge of yours in New Jersey?"

"Oh, that doesn't amount to anything. It's held up by a steel strike. A bother, of course, but the sort of thing one is always having to put up with. But the Moorlock Bridge is a continual anxiety. You see, the truth is, we are having to build pretty well to the strain limit up there. They've crowded me too much on the cost. It's all very well if everything goes well, but these estimates have never been used for anything of such length before. However, there's nothing to be done. They hold me to the scale I've used in shorter bridges. The last thing a bridge commission cares about is the kind of bridge you build."

When Bartley had finished dressing for dinner he went into his study, where he found his wife arranging flowers on his writing-table.

"These pink roses just came from Mrs. Hastings," she said, smiling, "and I am sure she meant them for you."

Bartley looked about with an air of satisfaction at the greens and the wreaths in the windows. "Have you a moment, Winifred? I have just now been thinking that this is our twelfth Christmas. Can you realize it?" He went up to the table and took her hands away from the flowers, drying them with his pocket handkerchief. "They've been awfully happy ones, all of them, haven't they?" He took her in his arms and bent back, lifting her a little and giving her a long kiss. "You are happy, aren't you Winifred? More than anything else in the world, I want you to be happy. Sometimes, of late, I've thought you looked as if you were troubled."

"No; it's only when you are troubled and harassed that I feel worried, Bartley. I wish you always seemed as you do to-night. But you don't, always." She looked earnestly and inquiringly into his eyes.

Alexander took her two hands from his shoulders and swung them back and forth in his own, laughing his big blond laugh.

"I'm growing older, my dear; that's what you feel. Now, may I show you something? I meant to save them until to-morrow, but I want you to wear them to-night." He took a little leather box out of his pocket and opened it. On the white velvet lay two long pendants of curiously worked gold, set with pearls. Winifred looked from the box to Bartley and exclaimed:--

"Where did you ever find such gold work, Bartley?"

"It's old Flemish. Isn't it fine?"

"They are the most beautiful things, dear. But, you know, I never wear earrings."

"Yes, yes, I know. But I want you to wear them. I have always wanted you to. So few women can. There must be a good ear, to begin with, and a nose"--he waved his hand--"above reproach. Most women look silly in them. They go only with faces like yours--very, very proud, and just a little hard."

Winifred laughed as she went over to the mirror and fitted the delicate springs to the lobes of her ears. "Oh, Bartley, that old foolishness about my being hard. It really hurts my feelings. But I must go down now. People are beginning to come."

Bartley drew her arm about his neck and went to the door with her. "Not hard to me, Winifred," he whispered. "Never, never hard to me."

Left alone, he paced up and down his study. He was at home again, among all the dear familiar things that spoke to him of so many happy years. His house to-night would be full of charming people, who liked and admired him. Yet all the time, underneath his pleasure and hopefulness and satisfaction, he was conscious of the vibration of an unnatural excitement. Amid this light and warmth and friendliness, he sometimes started and shuddered, as if some one had stepped on his grave. Something had broken loose in him of which he knew nothing except that it was sullen and powerful, and that it wrung and tortured him. Sometimes it came upon him softly, in enervating reveries. Sometimes it battered him like the cannon rolling in the hold of the vessel. Always, now, it brought with it a sense of quickened life, of stimulating danger. To-night it came upon him suddenly, as he was walking the floor, after his wife left him. It seemed impossible; he could not believe it. He glanced entreatingly at the door, as if to call her back. He heard voices in the hall below, and knew that he must go down. Going over to the window, he looked out at the lights across the river. How could this happen here, in his own house, among the things he loved? What was it that reached in out of the darkness and thrilled him? As he stood there he had a feeling that he would never escape. He shut his eyes and pressed his forehead against the cold window glass, breathing in the chill that came through it. "That this," he groaned, "that this should have happened to ME!"

On New Year's day a thaw set in, and during the night torrents of rain fell. In the morning, the morning of Alexander's departure for England, the river was streaked with fog and the rain drove hard against the windows of the breakfast-room. Alexander had finished his coffee and was pacing up and down. His wife sat at the table, watching him. She was pale and unnaturally calm. When Thomas brought the letters, Bartley sank into his chair and ran them over rapidly.

"Here's a note from old Wilson. He's safe back at his grind, and says he had a bully time. 'The memory of Mrs. Bartley will make my whole winter fragrant.' Just like him. He will go on getting measureless satisfaction out of you by his study fire. What a man he is for looking on at life!" Bartley sighed, pushed the letters back impatiently, and went over to the window. "This is a nasty sort of day to sail. I've a notion to call it off. Next week would be time enough."

"That would only mean starting twice. It wouldn't really help you out at all," Mrs. Alexander spoke soothingly. "And you'd come back late for all your engagements."

Bartley began jingling some loose coins in his pocket. "I wish things would let me rest. I'm tired of work, tired of people, tired of trailing about." He looked out at the storm-beaten river.

Winifred came up behind him and put a hand on his shoulder. "That's what you always say, poor Bartley! At bottom you really like all these things. Can't you remember that?"

He put his arm about her. "All the same, life runs smoothly enough with some people, and with me it's always a messy sort of patchwork. It's like the song; peace is where I am not. How can you face it all with so much fortitude?"

She looked at him with that clear gaze which Wilson had so much admired, which he had felt implied such high confidence and fearless pride. "Oh, I faced that long ago, when you were on your first bridge, up at old Allway. I knew then that your paths were not to be paths of peace, but I decided that I wanted to follow them."

Bartley and his wife stood silent for a long time; the fire crackled in the grate, the rain beat insistently upon the windows, and the sleepy Angora looked up at them curiously.

Presently Thomas made a discreet sound at the door. "Shall Edward bring down your trunks, sir?"

"Yes; they are ready. Tell him not to forget the big portfolio on the study table."

Thomas withdrew, closing the door softly. Bartley turned away from his wife, still holding her hand. "It never gets any easier, Winifred."

They both started at the sound of the carriage on the pavement outside. Alexander sat down and leaned his head on his hand. His wife bent over him. "Courage," she said gayly. Bartley rose and rang the bell. Thomas brought him his hat and stick and ulster. At the sight of these, the supercilious Angora moved restlessly, quitted her red cushion by the fire, and came up, waving her tail in vexation at these ominous indications of change. Alexander stooped to stroke her, and then plunged into his coat and drew on his gloves. His wife held his stick, smiling. Bartley smiled too, and his eyes cleared. "I'll work like the devil, Winifred, and be home again before you realize I've gone." He kissed her quickly several times, hurried out of the front door into the rain, and waved to her from the carriage window as the driver was starting his melancholy, dripping black horses. Alexander sat with his hands clenched on his knees. As the carriage turned up the hill, he lifted one hand and brought it down violently. "This time"--he spoke aloud and through his set teeth--"this time I'm going to end it!"

On the afternoon of the third day out, Alexander was sitting well to the stern, on the windward side where the chairs were few, his rugs over him and the collar of his fur-lined coat turned up about his ears. The weather had so far been dark and raw. For two hours he had been watching the low, dirty sky and the beating of the heavy rain upon the iron-colored sea. There was a long, oily swell that made exercise laborious. The decks smelled of damp woolens, and the air was so humid that drops of moisture kept gathering upon his hair and mustache. He seldom moved except to brush them away. The great open spaces made him passive and the restlessness of the water quieted him. He intended during the voyage to decide upon a course of action, but he held all this away from him for the present and lay in a blessed gray oblivion. Deep down in him somewhere his resolution was weakening and strengthening, ebbing and flowing. The thing that perturbed him went on as steadily as his pulse, but he was almost unconscious of it. He was submerged in the vast impersonal grayness about him, and at intervals the sidelong roll of the boat measured off time like the ticking of a clock. He felt released from everything that troubled and perplexed him. It was as if he had tricked and outwitted torturing memories, had actually managed to get on board without them. He thought of nothing at all. If his mind now and again picked a face out of the grayness, it was Lucius Wilson's, or the face of an old schoolmate, forgotten for years; or it was the slim outline of a favorite greyhound he used to hunt jack-rabbits with when he was a boy.

Toward six o'clock the wind rose and tugged at the tarpaulin and brought the swell higher. After dinner Alexander came back to the wet deck, piled his damp rugs over him again, and sat smoking, losing himself in the obliterating blackness and drowsing in the rush of the gale. Before he went below a few bright stars were pricked off between heavily moving masses of cloud.

The next morning was bright and mild, with a fresh breeze. Alexander felt the need of exercise even before he came out of his cabin. When he went on deck the sky was blue and blinding, with heavy whiffs of white cloud, smoke-colored at the edges, moving rapidly across it. The water was roughish, a cold, clear indigo breaking into whitecaps. Bartley walked for two hours, and then stretched himself in the sun until lunch-time.

In the afternoon he wrote a long letter to Winifred. Later, as he walked the deck through a splendid golden sunset, his spirits rose continually. It was agreeable to come to himself again after several days of numbness and torpor. He stayed out until the last tinge of violet had faded from the water. There was literally a taste of life on his lips as he sat down to dinner and ordered a bottle of champagne. He was late in finishing his dinner, and drank rather more wine than he had meant to. When he went above, the wind had risen and the deck was almost deserted. As he stepped out of the door a gale lifted his heavy fur coat about his shoulders. He fought his way up the deck with keen exhilaration. The moment he stepped, almost out of breath, behind the shelter of the stern, the wind was cut off, and he felt, like a rush of warm air, a sense of close and intimate companionship. He started back and tore his coat open as if something warm were actually clinging to him beneath it. He hurried up the deck and went into the saloon parlor, full of women who had retreated thither from the sharp wind. He threw himself upon them. He talked delightfully to the older ones and played accompaniments for the younger ones until the last sleepy girl had followed her mother below. Then he went into the smoking-room. He played bridge until two o'clock in the morning, and managed to lose a considerable sum of money without really noticing that he was doing so.

After the break of one fine day the weather was pretty consistently dull. When the low sky thinned a trifle, the pale white spot of a sun did no more than throw a bluish lustre on the water, giving it the dark brightness of newly cut lead. Through one after another of those gray days Alexander drowsed and mused, drinking in the grateful moisture. But the complete peace of the first part of the voyage was over. Sometimes he rose suddenly from his chair as if driven out, and paced the deck for hours. People noticed his propensity for walking in rough weather, and watched him curiously as he did his rounds. From his abstraction and the determined set of his jaw, they fancied he must be thinking about his bridge. Every one had heard of the new cantilever bridge in Canada.

But Alexander was not thinking about his work. After the fourth night out, when his will suddenly softened under his hands, he had been continually hammering away at himself. More and more often, when he first wakened in the morning or when he stepped into a warm place after being chilled on the deck, he felt a sudden painful delight at being nearer another shore. Sometimes when he was most despondent, when he thought himself worn out with this struggle, in a flash he was free of it and leaped into an overwhelming consciousness of himself. On the instant he felt that marvelous return of the impetuousness, the intense excitement, the increasing expectancy of youth.

CHAPTER VI

The last two days of the voyage Bartley found almost intolerable. The stop at Queenstown, the tedious passage up the Mersey, were things that he noted dimly through his growing impatience. He had planned to stop in Liverpool; but, instead, he took the boat train for London.

Emerging at Euston at half-past three o'clock in the afternoon, Alexander had his luggage sent to the Savoy and drove at once to Bedford Square. When Marie met him at the door, even her strong sense of the proprieties could not restrain her surprise and delight. She blushed and smiled and fumbled his card in her confusion before she ran upstairs. Alexander paced up and down the hallway, buttoning and unbuttoning his overcoat, until she returned and took him up to Hilda's living-room. The room was empty when he entered. A coal fire was crackling in the grate and the lamps were lit, for it was already beginning to grow dark outside. Alexander did not sit down. He stood his ground over by the windows until Hilda came in. She called his name on the threshold, but in her swift flight across the room she felt a change in him and caught herself up so deftly that he could not tell just when she did it. She merely brushed his cheek with her lips and put a hand lightly and joyously on either shoulder. "Oh, what a grand thing to happen on a raw day! I felt it in my bones when I woke this morning that something splendid was going to turn up. I thought it might be Sister Kate or Cousin Mike would be happening along. I never dreamed it would be you, Bartley. But why do you let me chatter on like this? Come over to the fire; you're chilled through."

She pushed him toward the big chair by the fire, and sat down on a stool at the opposite side of the hearth, her knees drawn up to her chin, laughing like a happy little girl.

"When did you come, Bartley, and how did it happen? You haven't spoken a word."

"I got in about ten minutes ago. I landed at Liverpool this morning and came down on the boat train."

Alexander leaned forward and warmed his hands before the blaze. Hilda watched him with perplexity.

"There's something troubling you, Bartley. What is it?"

Bartley bent lower over the fire. "It's the whole thing that troubles me, Hilda. You and I."

Hilda took a quick, soft breath. She looked at his heavy shoulders and big, determined head, thrust forward like a catapult in leash.

"What about us, Bartley?" she asked in a thin voice.

He locked and unlocked his hands over the grate and spread his fingers close to the bluish flame, while the coals crackled and the clock ticked and a street vendor began to call under the window. At last Alexander brought out one word:--

"Everything!"

Hilda was pale by this time, and her eyes were wide with fright. She looked about desperately from Bartley to the door, then to the windows, and back again to Bartley. She rose uncertainly, touched his hair with her hand, then sank back upon her stool.

"I'll do anything you wish me to, Bartley," she said tremulously. "I can't stand seeing you miserable."

"I can't live with myself any longer," he answered roughly.

He rose and pushed the chair behind him and began to walk miserably about the room, seeming to find it too small for him. He pulled up a window as if the air were heavy.

Hilda watched him from her corner, trembling and scarcely breathing, dark shadows growing about her eyes.

"It . . . it hasn't always made you miserable, has it?" Her eyelids fell and her lips quivered.

"Always. But it's worse now. It's unbearable. It tortures me every minute."

"But why NOW?" she asked piteously, wringing her hands.

He ignored her question. "I am not a man who can live two lives," he went on feverishly. "Each life spoils the other. I get nothing but misery out of either. The world is all there, just as it used to be, but I can't get at it any more. There is this deception between me and everything."

At that word "deception," spoken with such self-contempt, the color flashed back into Hilda's face as suddenly as if she had been struck by a whiplash. She bit her lip and looked down at her hands, which were clasped tightly in front of her.

"Could you--could you sit down and talk about it quietly, Bartley, as if I were a friend, and not some one who had to be defied?"

He dropped back heavily into his chair by the fire. "It was myself I was defying, Hilda. I have thought about it until I am worn out."

He looked at her and his haggard face softened. He put out his hand toward her as he looked away again into the fire.

She crept across to him, drawing her stool after her. "When did you first begin to feel like this, Bartley?"

"After the very first. The first was--sort of in play, wasn't it?"

Hilda's face quivered, but she whispered: "Yes, I think it must have been. But why didn't you tell me when you were here in the summer?"

Alexander groaned. "I meant to, but somehow I couldn't. We had only a few days, and your new play was just on, and you were so happy."

"Yes, I was happy, wasn't I?" She pressed his hand gently in gratitude. "Weren't you happy then, at all?"

She closed her eyes and took a deep breath, as if to draw in again the fragrance of those days. Something of their troubling sweetness came back to Alexander, too. He moved uneasily and his chair creaked.

"Yes, I was then. You know. But afterward. . ."

"Yes, yes," she hurried, pulling her hand gently away from him. Presently it stole back to his coat sleeve. "Please tell me one thing, Bartley. At least, tell me that you believe I thought I was making you happy."

His hand shut down quickly over the questioning fingers on his sleeves. "Yes, Hilda; I know that," he said simply.

She leaned her head against his arm and spoke softly:--

"You see, my mistake was in wanting you to have everything. I wanted you to eat all the cakes and have them, too. I somehow believed that I could take all the bad consequences for you. I wanted you always to be happy and handsome and successful--to have all the things that a great man ought to have, and, once in a way, the careless holidays that great men are not permitted."

Bartley gave a bitter little laugh, and Hilda looked up and read in the deepening lines of his face that youth and Bartley would not much longer struggle together.

"I understand, Bartley. I was wrong. But I didn't know. You've only to tell me now. What must I do that I've not done, or what must I not do?" She listened intently, but she heard nothing but the creaking of his chair. "You want me to say it?" she whispered. "You want to tell me that you can only see me like this, as old friends do, or out in the world among people? I can do that."

"I can't," he said heavily.

Hilda shivered and sat still. Bartley leaned his head in his hands and spoke through his teeth. "It's got to be a clean break, Hilda. I can't see you at all, any-where. What I mean is that I want you to promise never to see me again, no matter how often I come, no matter how hard I beg."

Hilda sprang up like a flame. She stood over him with her hands clenched at her side, her body rigid.

"No!" she gasped. "It's too late to ask that. Do you hear me, Bartley? It's too late. I won't promise. It's abominable of you to ask me. Keep away if you wish; when have I ever followed you? But, if you come to me, I'll do as I see fit. The shame-fulness of your asking me to do that! If you come to me, I'll do as I see fit. Do you understand? Bartley, you're cowardly!"

Alexander rose and shook himself angrily. "Yes, I know I'm cowardly. I'm afraid of myself. I don't trust myself any more. I carried it all lightly enough at first, but now I don't dare trifle with it. It's getting the better of me. It's different now. I'm growing older, and you've got my young self here with you. It's through him that I've come to wish for you all and all the time." He took her roughly in his arms. "Do you know what I mean?"

Hilda held her face back from him and began to cry bitterly. "Oh, Bartley, what am I to do? Why didn't you let me be angry with you? You ask me to stay away from you because you want me! And I've got nobody but you. I will do anything you say--but that! I will ask the least imaginable, but I must have SOMETHING!"

Bartley turned away and sank down in his chair again. Hilda sat on the arm of it and put her hands lightly on his shoulders.

"Just something Bartley. I must have you to think of through the months and months of loneliness. I must see you. I must know about you. The sight of you, Bartley, to see you living and happy and successful--can I never make you understand what that means to me?" She pressed his shoulders gently. "You see, loving some one as I love you makes the whole world different. If I'd met you later, if I hadn't loved you so well--but that's all over, long ago. Then came all those years without you, lonely and hurt and discouraged; those decent young fellows and poor Mac, and me never heeding--hard as a steel spring. And then you came back, not caring very much, but it made no difference."

She slid to the floor beside him, as if she were too tired to sit up any longer. Bartley bent over and took her in his arms, kissing her mouth and her wet, tired eyes.

"Don't cry, don't cry," he whispered. "We've tortured each other enough for tonight. Forget everything except that I am here."

"I think I have forgotten everything but that already," she murmured. "Ah, your dear arms!"

CHAPTER VII

During the fortnight that Alexander was in London he drove himself hard. He got through a great deal of personal business and saw a great many men who were doing interesting things in his own profession. He disliked to think of his visits to London as holidays, and when he was there he worked even harder than he did at home.

The day before his departure for Liverpool was a singularly fine one. The thick air had cleared overnight in a strong wind which brought in a golden dawn and then fell off to a fresh breeze. When Bartley looked out of his windows from the Savoy, the river was flashing silver and the gray stone along the Embankment was bathed in bright, clear sunshine. London had wakened to life after three weeks of cold and sodden rain. Bartley breakfasted hurriedly and went over his mail while the hotel valet packed his trunks. Then he paid his account and walked rapidly down the Strand past Charing Cross Station. His spirits rose with every step, and when he reached Trafalgar Square, blazing in the sun, with its fountains playing and its column reaching up into the bright air, he signaled to a hansom, and, before he knew what he was about, told the driver to go to Bedford Square by way of the British Museum.

When he reached Hilda's apartment she met him, fresh as the morning itself. Her rooms were flooded with sunshine and full of the flowers he had been sending her. She would never let him give her anything else.

"Are you busy this morning, Hilda?" he asked as he sat down, his hat and gloves in his hand.

"Very. I've been up and about three hours, working at my part. We open in February, you know."

"Well, then you've worked enough. And so have I. I've seen all my men, my packing is done, and I go up to Liverpool this evening. But this morning we are going to have a holiday. What do you say to a drive out to Kew and Richmond? You may not get another day like this all winter. It's like a fine April day at home. May I use your telephone? I want to order the carriage."

"Oh, how jolly! There, sit down at the desk. And while you are telephoning I'll change my dress. I shan't be long. All the morning papers are on the table."

Hilda was back in a few moments wearing a long gray squirrel coat and a broad fur hat.

Bartley rose and inspected her. "Why don't you wear some of those pink roses?" he asked.

"But they came only this morning, and they have not even begun to open. I was saving them. I am so unconsciously thrifty!" She laughed as she looked about the room. "You've been sending me far too many flowers, Bartley. New ones every day. That's too often; though I do love to open the boxes, and I take good care of them."

"Why won't you let me send you any of those jade or ivory things you are so fond of? Or pictures? I know a good deal about pictures."

Hilda shook her large hat as she drew the roses out of the tall glass. "No, there are some things you can't do. There's the carriage. Will you button my gloves for me?"

Bartley took her wrist and began to button the long gray suede glove. "How gay your eyes are this morning, Hilda."

"That's because I've been studying. It always stirs me up a little."

He pushed the top of the glove up slowly. "When did you learn to take hold of your parts like that?"

"When I had nothing else to think of. Come, the carriage is waiting. What a shocking while you take."

"I'm in no hurry. We've plenty of time."

They found all London abroad. Piccadilly was a stream of rapidly moving carriages, from which flashed furs and flowers and bright winter costumes. The metal trappings of the harnesses shone dazzlingly, and the wheels were revolving disks that threw off rays of light. The parks were full of children and nursemaids and joyful dogs that leaped and yelped and scratched up the brown earth with their paws.

"I'm not going until to-morrow, you know," Bartley announced suddenly. "I'll cut off a day in Liverpool. I haven't felt so jolly this long while."

Hilda looked up with a smile which she tried not to make too glad. "I think people were meant to be happy, a little," she said.

They had lunch at Richmond and then walked to Twickenham, where they had sent the carriage. They drove back, with a glorious sunset behind them, toward the distant gold-washed city. It was one of those rare afternoons when all the thickness and shadow of London are changed to a kind of shining, pulsing, special atmosphere; when the smoky vapors become fluttering golden clouds, nacreous veils of pink and amber; when all that bleakness of gray stone and dullness of dirty brick trembles in aureate light, and all the roofs and spires, and one great dome, are floated in golden haze. On such rare afternoons the ugliest of cities becomes the most poetic, and months of sodden days are offset by a moment of miracle.

"It's like that with us Londoners, too," Hilda was saying. "Everything is awfully grim and cheerless, our weather and our houses and our ways of amusing ourselves. But we can be happier than anybody. We can go mad with joy, as the people do out in the fields on a fine Whitsunday. We make the most of our moment."

She thrust her little chin out defiantly over her gray fur collar, and Bartley looked down at her and laughed.

"You are a plucky one, you." He patted her glove with his hand. "Yes, you are a plucky one."

Hilda sighed. "No, I'm not. Not about some things, at any rate. It doesn't take pluck to fight for one's moment, but it takes pluck to go without--a lot. More than I have. I can't help it," she added fiercely.

After miles of outlying streets and little gloomy houses, they reached London itself, red and roaring and murky, with a thick dampness coming up from the river, that betokened fog again to-morrow. The streets were full of people who had worked indoors all through the priceless day and had now come hungrily out to drink the muddy lees of it. They stood in long black lines, waiting before the pit entrances of the theatres--short-coated boys, and girls in sailor hats, all shivering and chatting gayly. There was a blurred rhythm in all the dull city noises--in the clatter of the cab horses and the rumbling of the busses, in the street calls, and in the undulating tramp, tramp of the crowd. It was like the deep vibration of some vast underground machinery, and like the muffled pulsations of millions of human hearts[1].

"Seems good to get back, doesn't it?" Bartley whispered, as they drove from Bayswater Road into Oxford Street. "London always makes me want to live more than any other city in the world. You remember our priestess mummy over in the mummy-room, and how we used to long to go and bring her out on nights like this? Three thousand years! Ugh!"

"All the same, I believe she used to feel it when we stood there and watched her and wished her well. I believe she used to remember," Hilda said thoughtfully.

"I hope so. Now let's go to some awfully jolly place for dinner before we go home. I could eat all the dinners there are in London to-night. Where shall I tell the driver? The Piccadilly Restaurant? The music's good there."

"There are too many people there whom one knows. Why not that little French place in Soho, where we went so often when you were here in the summer? I love it, and I've never been there with any one but you. Sometimes I go by myself, when I am particularly lonely."

"Very well, the sole's good there. How many street pianos there are about to-night! The fine weather must have thawed them out. We've had five miles of `Il Trovatore' now. They always make me feel jaunty. Are you comfy, and not too tired?"

"I'm not tired at all. I was just wondering how people can ever die. Why did you remind me of the mummy? Life seems the strongest and most indestructible thing in the world. Do you really believe that all those people rushing about down there, going to good dinners and clubs and theatres, will be dead some day, and not care about anything? I don't believe it, and I know I shan't die, ever! You see, I feel too--too powerful!"

The carriage stopped. Bartley sprang out and swung her quickly to the pavement. As he lifted her in his two hands he whispered: "You are--powerful!"

---

1 See "The Barrel Organ by Alfred Noyes. Ed.

CHAPTER VIII

The last rehearsal was over, a tedious dress rehearsal which had lasted all day and exhausted the patience of every one who had to do with it. When Hilda had dressed for the street and came out of her dressing-room, she found Hugh MacConnell waiting for her in the corridor.

"The fog's thicker than ever, Hilda. There have been a great many accidents to-day. It's positively unsafe for you to be out alone. Will you let me take you home?"

"How good of you, Mac. If you are going with me, I think I'd rather walk. I've had no exercise to-day, and all this has made me nervous."

"I shouldn't wonder," said MacConnell dryly. Hilda pulled down her veil and they stepped out into the thick brown wash that submerged St. Martin's Lane. Mac-Connell took her hand and tucked it snugly under his arm. "I'm sorry I was such a savage. I hope you didn't think I made an ass of myself."

"Not a bit of it. I don't wonder you were peppery. Those things are awfully trying. How do you think it's going?"

"Magnificently. That's why I got so stirred up. We are going to hear from this, both of us. And that reminds me; I've got news for you. They are going to begin repairs on the theatre about the middle of March, and we are to run over to New York for six weeks. Bennett told me yesterday that it was decided."

Hilda looked up delightedly at the tall gray figure beside her. He was the only thing she could see, for they were moving through a dense opaqueness, as if they were walking at the bottom of the ocean.

"Oh, Mac, how glad I am! And they love your things over there, don't they?"

"Shall you be glad for--any other reason, Hilda?"

MacConnell put his hand in front of her to ward off some dark object. It proved to be only a lamp-post, and they beat in farther from the edge of the pavement.

"What do you mean, Mac?" Hilda asked nervously.

"I was just thinking there might be people over there you'd be glad to see," he brought out awkwardly. Hilda said nothing, and as they walked on MacConnell spoke again, apologetically: "I hope you don't mind my knowing about it, Hilda. Don't stiffen up like that. No one else knows, and I didn't try to find out anything. I felt it, even before I knew who he was. I knew there was somebody, and that it wasn't I."

They crossed Oxford Street in silence, feeling their way. The busses had stopped running and the cab-drivers were leading their horses. When they reached the other side, MacConnell said suddenly, "I hope you are happy."

"Terribly, dangerously happy, Mac,"--Hilda spoke quietly, pressing the rough sleeve of his greatcoat with her gloved hand.

"You've always thought me too old for you, Hilda,--oh, of course you've never said just that,--and here this fellow is not more than eight years younger than I. I've always felt that if I could get out of my old case I might win you yet. It's a fine, brave youth I carry inside me, only he'll never be seen."

"Nonsense, Mac. That has nothing to do with it. It's because you seem too close to me, too much my own kind. It would be like marrying Cousin Mike, almost. I really tried to care as you wanted me to, away back in the beginning."

"Well, here we are, turning out of the Square. You are not angry with me, Hilda? Thank you for this walk, my dear. Go in and get dry things on at once. You'll be having a great night to-morrow."

She put out her hand. "Thank you, Mac, for everything. Good-night."

MacConnell trudged off through the fog, and she went slowly upstairs. Her slippers and dressing gown were waiting for her before the fire. "I shall certainly see him in New York. He will see by the papers that we are coming. Perhaps he knows it already," Hilda kept thinking as she undressed. "Perhaps he will be at the dock. No, scarcely that; but I may meet him in the street even before he comes to see me." Marie placed the tea-table by the fire and brought Hilda her letters. She looked them over, and started as she came to one in a handwriting that she did not often see; Alexander had written to her only twice before, and he did not allow her to write to him at all. "Thank you, Marie. You may go now."

Hilda sat down by the table with the letter in her hand, still unopened. She looked at it intently, turned it over, and felt its thickness with her fingers. She believed that she sometimes had a kind of second-sight about letters, and could tell before she read them whether they brought good or evil tidings. She put this one down on the table in front of her while she poured her tea. At last, with a little shiver of expectancy, she tore open the envelope and read:--

Boston, February --

MY DEAR HILDA:--

It is after twelve o'clock. Every one else is in bed and I am sitting alone in my study. I have been happier in this room than anywhere else in the world. Happiness like that makes one insolent. I used to think these four walls could stand against anything. And now I scarcely know myself here. Now I know that no one can build his security upon the nobleness of another person. Two people, when they love each other, grow alike in their tastes and habits and pride, but their moral natures (whatever we may mean by that canting expression) are never welded. The base one goes on being base, and the noble one noble, to the end.

The last week has been a bad one; I have been realizing how things used to be with me. Sometimes I get used to being dead inside, but lately it has been as if a window beside me had suddenly opened, and as if all the smells of spring blew in to me. There is a garden out there, with stars overhead, where I used to walk at night when I had a single purpose and a single heart. I can remember how I used to feel there, how beautiful everything about me was, and what life and power and freedom I felt in myself. When the window opens I know exactly how it would feel to be out there. But that garden is closed to me. How is it, I ask myself, that everything can be so different with me when nothing here has changed? I am in my own house, in my own study, in the midst of all these quiet streets where my friends live. They are all safe and at peace with themselves. But I am never at peace. I feel always on the edge of danger and change.

I keep remembering locoed horses I used to see on the range when I was a boy. They changed like that. We used to catch them and put them up in the corral, and they developed great cunning. They would pretend to eat their oats like the other horses, but we knew they were always scheming to get back at the loco.

It seems that a man is meant to live only one life in this world. When he tries to live a second, he develops another nature. I feel as if a second man had been grafted into me. At first he seemed only a pleasure-loving simpleton, of whose company I was rather ashamed, and whom I used to hide under my coat when I walked the Embankment, in London. But now he is strong and sullen, and he is fighting for his life at the cost of mine. That is his one activity: to grow strong. No creature ever wanted so much to live. Eventually, I suppose, he will absorb me altogether. Believe me, you will hate me then.

And what have you to do, Hilda, with this ugly story? Nothing at all. The little boy drank of the prettiest brook in the forest and he became a stag. I write all this because I can never tell it to you, and because it seems as if I could not keep silent any longer. And because I suffer, Hilda. If any one I loved suffered like this, I'd want to know it. Help me, Hilda!

B.A.

CHAPTER IX

On the last Saturday in April, the New York "Times" published an account of the strike complications which were delaying Alexander's New Jersey bridge, and stated that the engineer himself was in town and at his office on West Tenth Street.

On Sunday, the day after this notice appeared, Alexander worked all day at his Tenth Street rooms. His business often called him to New York, and he had kept an apartment there for years, subletting it when he went abroad for any length of time. Besides his sleeping-room and bath, there was a large room, formerly a painter's studio, which he used as a study and office. It was furnished with the cast-off possessions of his bachelor days and with odd things which he sheltered for friends of his who followed itinerant and more or less artistic callings. Over the fireplace there was a large old-fashioned gilt mirror. Alexander's big work-table stood in front of one of the three windows, and above the couch hung the one picture in the room, a big canvas of charming color and spirit, a study of the Luxembourg Gardens in early spring, painted in his youth by a man who had since become a portrait-painter of international renown. He had done it for Alexander when they were students together in Paris.

Sunday was a cold, raw day and a fine rain fell continuously. When Alexander came back from dinner he put more wood on his fire, made himself comfortable, and settled down at his desk, where he began checking over estimate sheets. It was after nine o'clock and he was lighting a second pipe, when he thought he heard a sound at his door. He started and listened, holding the burning match in his hand; again he heard the same sound, like a firm, light tap. He rose and crossed the room quickly. When he threw open the door he recognized the figure that shrank back into the bare, dimly lit hallway. He stood for a moment in awkward constraint, his pipe in his hand.

"Come in," he said to Hilda at last, and closed the door behind her. He pointed to a chair by the fire and went back to his worktable. "Won't you sit down?"

He was standing behind the table, turning over a pile of blueprints nervously. The yellow light from the student's lamp fell on his hands and the purple sleeves of his velvet smoking-jacket, but his flushed face and big, hard head were in the shadow. There was something about him that made Hilda wish herself at her hotel again, in the street below, anywhere but where she was.

"Of course I know, Bartley," she said at last, "that after this you won't owe me the least consideration. But we sail on Tuesday. I saw that interview in the paper yesterday, telling where you were, and I thought I had to see you. That's all. Good-night; I'm going now." She turned and her hand closed on the door-knob.

Alexander hurried toward her and took her gently by the arm. "Sit down, Hilda; you're wet through. Let me take off your coat--and your boots; they're oozing water." He knelt down and began to unlace her shoes, while Hilda shrank into the chair. "Here, put your feet on this stool. You don't mean to say you walked down--and without overshoes!"

Hilda hid her face in her hands. "I was afraid to take a cab. Can't you see, Bartley, that I'm terribly frightened? I've been through this a hundred times to-day. Don't be any more angry than you can help. I was all right until I knew you were in town. If you'd sent me a note, or telephoned me, or anything! But you won't let me write to you, and I had to see you after that letter, that terrible letter you wrote me when you got home."

Alexander faced her, resting his arm on the mantel behind him, and began to brush the sleeve of his jacket. "Is this the way you mean to answer it, Hilda?" he asked unsteadily.

She was afraid to look up at him. "Didn't--didn't you mean even to say goodby to me, Bartley? Did you mean just to--quit me?" she asked. "I came to tell you that I'm willing to do as you asked me. But it's no use talking about that now. Give me my things, please." She put her hand out toward the fender.

Alexander sat down on the arm of her chair. "Did you think I had forgotten you were in town, Hilda? Do you think I kept away by accident? Did you suppose I didn't know you were sailing on Tuesday? There is a letter for you there, in my desk drawer. It was to have reached you on the steamer. I was all the morning writing it. I told myself that if I were really thinking of you, and not of myself, a letter would be better than nothing. Marks on paper mean something to you." He paused. "They never did to me."

Hilda smiled up at him beautifully and put her hand on his sleeve. "Oh, Bartley! Did you write to me? Why didn't you telephone me to let me know that you had? Then I wouldn't have come."

Alexander slipped his arm about her. "I didn't know it before, Hilda, on my honor I didn't, but I believe it was because, deep down in me somewhere, I was hoping I might drive you to do just this. I've watched that door all day. I've jumped up if the fire crackled. I think I have felt that you were coming." He bent his face over her hair.

"And I," she whispered,--"I felt that you were feeling that. But when I came, I thought I had been mistaken."

Alexander started up and began to walk up and down the room.

"No, you weren't mistaken. I've been up in Canada with my bridge, and I arranged not to come to New York until after you had gone. Then, when your manager added two more weeks, I was already committed." He dropped upon the stool in front of her and sat with his hands hanging between his knees. "What am I to do, Hilda?"

"That's what I wanted to see you about, Bartley. I'm going to do what you asked me to do when you were in London. Only I'll do it more completely. I'm going to marry."

"Who?"

"Oh, it doesn't matter much! One of them. Only not Mac. I'm too fond of him."

Alexander moved restlessly. "Are you joking, Hilda?"

"Indeed I'm not."

"Then you don't know what you're talking about."

"Yes, I know very well. I've thought about it a great deal, and I've quite decided. I never used to understand how women did things like that, but I know now. It's because they can't be at the mercy of the man they love any longer."

Alexander flushed angrily. "So it's better to be at the mercy of a man you don't love?"

"Under such circumstances, infinitely!"

There was a flash in her eyes that made Alexander's fall. He got up and went over to the window, threw it open, and leaned out. He heard Hilda moving about behind him. When he looked over his shoulder she was lacing her boots. He went back and stood over her.

"Hilda you'd better think a while longer before you do that. I don't know what I ought to say, but I don't believe you'd be happy; truly I don't. Aren't you trying to frighten me?"

She tied the knot of the last lacing and put her boot-heel down firmly. "No; I'm telling you what I've made up my mind to do. I suppose I would better do it without telling you. But afterward I shan't have an opportunity to explain, for I shan't be seeing you again."

Alexander started to speak, but caught himself. When Hilda rose he sat down on the arm of her chair and drew her back into it.

"I wouldn't be so much alarmed if I didn't know how utterly reckless you CAN be. Don't do anything like that rashly." His face grew troubled. "You wouldn't be happy. You are not that kind of woman. I'd never have another hour's peace if I helped to make you do a thing like that." He took her face between his hands and looked down into it. "You see, you are different, Hilda. Don't you know you are?" His voice grew softer, his touch more and more tender. "Some women can do that sort of thing, but you--you can love as queens did, in the old time."

Hilda had heard that soft, deep tone in his voice only once before. She closed her eyes; her lips and eyelids trembled. "Only one, Bartley. Only one. And he threw it back at me a second time."

She felt the strength leap in the arms that held her so lightly.

"Try him again, Hilda. Try him once again."

She looked up into his eyes, and hid her face in her hands.

CHAPTER X

On Tuesday afternoon a Boston lawyer, who had been trying a case in Vermont, was standing on the siding at White River Junction when the Canadian Express pulled by on its northward journey. As the day-coaches at the rear end of the long train swept by him, the lawyer noticed at one of the windows a man's head, with thick rumpled hair. "Curious," he thought; "that looked like Alexander, but what would he be doing back there in the daycoaches?"

It was, indeed, Alexander.

That morning a telegram from Moorlock had reached him, telling him that there was serious trouble with the bridge and that he was needed there at once, so he had caught the first train out of New York. He had taken a seat in a day-coach to avoid the risk of meeting any one he knew, and because he did not wish to be comfortable. When the telegram arrived, Alexander was at his rooms on Tenth Street, packing his bag to go to Boston. On Monday night he had written a long letter to his wife, but when morning came he was afraid to send it, and the letter was still in his pocket. Winifred was not a woman who could bear disappointment. She demanded a great deal of herself and of the people she loved; and she never failed herself. If he told her now, he knew, it would be irretrievable. There would be no going back. He would lose the thing he valued most in the world; he would be destroying himself and his own happiness. There would be nothing for him afterward. He seemed to see himself dragging out a restless existence on the Continent--Cannes, Hyeres, Algiers, Cairo--among smartly dressed, disabled men of every nationality; forever going on journeys that led nowhere; hurrying to catch trains that he might just as well miss; getting up in the morning with a great bustle and splashing of water, to begin a day that had no purpose and no meaning; dining late to shorten the night, sleeping late to shorten the day.

And for what? For a mere folly, a masquerade, a little thing that he could not let go. AND HE COULD EVEN LET IT GO, he told himself. But he had promised to be in London at mid-summer, and he knew that he would go. . . . It was impossible to live like this any longer.

And this, then, was to be the disaster that his old professor had foreseen for him: the crack in the wall, the crash, the cloud of dust. And he could not understand how it had come about. He felt that he himself was unchanged, that he was still there, the same man he had been five years ago, and that he was sitting stupidly by and letting some resolute offshoot of himself spoil his life for him. This new force was not he, it was but a part of him. He would not even admit that it was stronger than he; but it was more active. It was by its energy that this new feeling got the better of him. His wife was the woman who had made his life, gratified his pride, given direction to his tastes and habits. The life they led together seemed to him beautiful. Winifred still was, as she had always been, Romance for him, and whenever he was deeply stirred he turned to her. When the grandeur and beauty of the world challenged him--as it challenges even the most self-absorbed people--he always answered with her name. That was his reply to the question put by the mountains and the stars; to all the spiritual aspects of life. In his feeling for his wife there was all the tenderness, all the pride, all the devotion of which he was capable. There was everything but energy; the energy of youth which must register itself and cut its name before it passes. This new feeling was so fresh, so unsatisfied and light of foot. It ran and was not wearied, anticipated him everywhere. It put a girdle round the earth while he was going from New York to Moorlock. At this moment, it was tingling through him, exultant, and live as quicksilver, whispering, "In July you will be in England."

Already he dreaded the long, empty days at sea, the monotonous Irish coast, the sluggish passage up the Mersey, the flash of the boat train through the summer country. He closed his eyes and gave himself up to the feeling of rapid motion and to swift, terrifying thoughts. He was sitting so, his face shaded by his hand, when the Boston lawyer saw him from the siding at White River Junction.

When at last Alexander roused himself, the afternoon had waned to sunset. The train was passing through a gray country and the sky overhead was flushed with a wide flood of clear color. There was a rose-colored light over the gray rocks and hills and meadows. Off to the left, under the approach of a weather-stained wooden bridge, a group of boys were sitting around a little fire. The smell of the wood smoke blew in at the window. Except for an old farmer, jogging along the highroad in his box-wagon, there was not another living creature to be seen. Alexander looked back wistfully at the boys, camped on the edge of a little marsh, crouching under their shelter and looking gravely at their fire. They took his mind back a long way, to a campfire on a sandbar in a Western river, and he wished he could go back and sit down with them. He could remember exactly how the world had looked then.

It was quite dark and Alexander was still thinking of the boys, when it occurred to him that the train must be nearing Allway. In going to his new bridge at Moorlock he had always to pass through Allway. The train stopped at Allway Mills, then wound two miles up the river, and then the hollow sound under his feet told Bartley that he was on his first bridge again. The bridge seemed longer than it had ever seemed before, and he was glad when he felt the beat of the wheels on the solid roadbed again. He did not like coming and going across that bridge, or remembering the man who built it. And was he, indeed, the same man who used to walk that bridge at night, promising such things to himself and to the stars? And yet, he could remember it all so well: the quiet hills sleeping in the moonlight, the slender skeleton of the bridge reaching out into the river, and up yonder, alone on the hill, the big white house; upstairs, in Winifred's window, the light that told him she was still awake and still thinking of him. And after the light went out he walked alone, taking the heavens into his confidence, unable to tear himself away from the white magic of the night, unwilling to sleep because longing was so sweet to him, and because, for the first time since first the hills were hung with moonlight, there was a lover in the world. And always there was the sound of the rushing water underneath, the sound which, more than anything else, meant death; the wearing away of things under the impact of physical forces which men could direct but never circumvent or diminish. Then, in the exaltation of love, more than ever it seemed to him to mean death, the only other thing as strong as love. Under the moon, under the cold, splendid stars, there were only those two things awake and sleepless; death and love, the rushing river and his burning heart.

Alexander sat up and looked about him. The train was tearing on through the darkness. All his companions in the day-coach were either dozing or sleeping heavily, and the murky lamps were turned low. How came he here among all these dirty people? Why was he going to London? What did it mean--what was the answer? How could this happen to a man who had lived through that magical spring and summer, and who had felt that the stars themselves were but flaming particles in the far-away infinitudes of his love?

What had he done to lose it? How could he endure the baseness of life without it? And with every revolution of the wheels beneath him, the unquiet quicksilver in his breast told him that at midsummer he would be in London. He remembered his last night there: the red foggy darkness, the hungry crowds before the theatres, the hand-organs, the feverish rhythm of the blurred, crowded streets, and the feeling of letting himself go with the crowd. He shuddered and looked about him at the poor unconscious companions of his journey, unkempt and travel-stained, now doubled in unlovely attitudes, who had come to stand to him for the ugliness he had brought into the world.

And those boys back there, beginning it all just as he had begun it; he wished he could promise them better luck. Ah, if one could promise any one better luck, if one could assure a single human being of happiness! He had thought he could do so, once; and it was thinking of that that he at last fell asleep. In his sleep, as if it had nothing fresher to work upon, his mind went back and tortured itself with something years and years away, an old, long-forgotten sorrow of his childhood.

When Alexander awoke in the morning, the sun was just rising through pale golden ripples of cloud, and the fresh yellow light was vibrating through the pine woods. The white birches, with their little unfolding leaves, gleamed in the lowlands, and the marsh meadows were already coming to life with their first green, a thin, bright color which had run over them like fire. As the train rushed along the trestles, thousands of wild birds rose screaming into the light. The sky was already a pale blue and of the clearness of crystal. Bartley caught up his bag and hurried through the Pullman coaches until he found the conductor. There was a stateroom unoccupied, and he took it and set about changing his clothes. Last night he would not have believed that anything could be so pleasant as the cold water he dashed over his head and shoulders and the freshness of clean linen on his body.

After he had dressed, Alexander sat down at the window and drew into his lungs deep breaths of the pine-scented air. He had awakened with all his old sense of power. He could not believe that things were as bad with him as they had seemed last night, that there was no way to set them entirely right. Even if he went to London at midsummer, what would that mean except that he was a fool? And he had been a fool before. That was not the reality of his life. Yet he knew that he would go to London.

Half an hour later the train stopped at Moorlock. Alexander sprang to the platform and hurried up the siding, waving to Philip Horton, one of his assistants, who was anxiously looking up at the windows of the coaches. Bartley took his arm and they went together into the station buffet.

"I'll have my coffee first, Philip. Have you had yours? And now, what seems to be the matter up here?"

The young man, in a hurried, nervous way, began his explanation.

But Alexander cut him short. "When did you stop work?" he asked sharply.

The young engineer looked confused. "I haven't stopped work yet, Mr. Alexander. I didn't feel that I could go so far without definite authorization from you."

"Then why didn't you say in your telegram exactly what you thought, and ask for your authorization? You'd have got it quick enough."

"Well, really, Mr. Alexander, I couldn't be absolutely sure, you know, and I didn't like to take the responsibility of making it public."

Alexander pushed back his chair and rose. "Anything I do can be made public, Phil. You say that you believe the lower chords are showing strain, and that even the workmen have been talking about it, and yet you've gone on adding weight."

"I'm sorry, Mr. Alexander, but I had counted on your getting here yesterday. My first telegram missed you somehow. I sent one Sunday evening, to the same address, but it was returned to me."

"Have you a carriage out there? I must stop to send a wire."

Alexander went up to the telegraph-desk and penciled the following message to his wife:--

I may have to be here for some time. Can you come up at once? Urgent.
BARTLEY.

The Moorlock Bridge lay three miles above the town. When they were seated in the carriage, Alexander began to question his assistant further. If it were true that the compression members showed strain, with the bridge only two thirds done, then there was nothing to do but pull the whole structure down and begin over again. Horton kept repeating that he was sure there could be nothing wrong with the estimates.

Alexander grew impatient. "That's all true, Phil, but we never were justified in assuming that a scale that was perfectly safe for an ordinary bridge would work with anything of such length. It's all very well on paper, but it remains to be seen whether it can be done in practice. I should have thrown up the job when they crowded me. It's all nonsense to try to do what other engineers are doing when you know they're not sound."

"But just now, when there is such competition," the younger man demurred. "And certainly that's the new line of development."

Alexander shrugged his shoulders and made no reply.

When they reached the bridge works, Alexander began his examination immediately. An hour later he sent for the superintendent. "I think you had better stop work out there at once, Dan. I should say that the lower chord here might buckle at any moment. I told the Commission that we were using higher unit stresses than any practice has established, and we've put the dead load at a low estimate. Theoretically it worked out well enough, but it had never actually been tried." Alexander put on his overcoat and took the superintendent by the arm. "Don't look so chopfallen, Dan. It's a jolt, but we've got to face it. It isn't the end of the world, you know. Now we'll go out and call the men off quietly. They're already nervous, Horton tells me, and there's no use alarming them. I'll go with you, and we'll send the end riveters in first."

Alexander and the superintendent picked their way out slowly over the long span. They went deliberately, stopping to see what each gang was doing, as if they were on an ordinary round of inspection. When they reached the end of the river span, Alexander nodded to the superintendent, who quietly gave an order to the foreman. The men in the end gang picked up their tools and, glancing curiously at each other, started back across the bridge toward the river-bank. Alexander himself remained standing where they had been working, looking about him. It was hard to believe, as he looked back over it, that the whole great span was incurably disabled, was already as good as condemned, because something was out of line in the lower chord of the cantilever arm.

The end riveters had reached the bank and were dispersing among the tool-houses, and the second gang had picked up their tools and were starting toward the shore. Alexander, still standing at the end of the river span, saw the lower chord of the cantilever arm give a little, like an elbow bending. He shouted and ran after the second gang, but by this time every one knew that the big river span was slowly settling. There was a burst of shouting that was immediately drowned by the scream and cracking of tearing iron, as all the tension work began to pull asunder. Once the chords began to buckle, there were thousands of tons of ironwork, all riveted together and lying in midair without support. It tore itself to pieces with roaring and grinding and noises that were like the shrieks of a steam whistle. There was no shock of any kind; the bridge had no impetus except from its own weight. It lurched neither to right nor left, but sank almost in a vertical line, snapping and breaking and tearing as it went, because no integral part could bear for an instant the enormous strain loosed upon it. Some of the men jumped and some ran, trying to make the shore.

At the first shriek of the tearing iron, Alexander jumped from the downstream side of the bridge. He struck the water without injury and disappeared. He was under the river a long time and had great difficulty in holding his breath. When it seemed impossible, and his chest was about to heave, he thought he heard his wife telling him that he could hold out a little longer. An instant later his face cleared the water. For a moment, in the depths of the river, he had realized what it would mean to die a hypocrite, and to lie dead under the last abandonment of her tenderness. But once in the light and air, he knew he should live to tell her and to recover all he had lost. Now, at last, he felt sure of himself. He was not startled. It seemed to him that he had been through something of this sort before. There was nothing horrible about it. This, too, was life, and life was activity, just as it was in Boston or in London. He was himself, and there was something to be done; everything seemed perfectly natural. Alexander was a strong swimmer, but he had gone scarcely a dozen strokes when the bridge itself, which had been settling faster and faster, crashed into the water behind him. Immediately the river was full of drowning men. A gang of French Canadians fell almost on top of him. He thought he had cleared them, when they began coming up all around him, clutching at him and at each other. Some of them could swim, but they were either hurt or crazed with fright. Alexander tried to beat them off, but there were too many of them. One caught him about the neck, another gripped him about the middle, and they went down together. When he sank, his wife seemed to be there in the water beside him, telling him to keep his head, that if he could hold out the men would drown and release him. There was something he wanted to tell his wife, but he could not think clearly for the roaring in his ears. Suddenly he remembered what it was. He caught his breath, and then she let him go.

The work of recovering the dead went on all day and all the following night. By the next morning forty-eight bodies had been taken out of the river, but there were still twenty missing. Many of the men had fallen with the bridge and were held down under the debris. Early on the morning of the second day a closed carriage was driven slowly along the river-bank and stopped a little below the works, where the river boiled and churned about the great iron carcass which lay in a straight line two thirds across it. The carriage stood there hour after hour, and word soon spread among the crowds on the shore that its occupant was the wife of the Chief Engineer; his body had not yet been found. The widows of the lost workmen, moving up and down the bank with shawls over their heads, some of them carrying babies, looked at the rusty hired hack many times that morning. They drew near it and walked about it, but none of them ventured to peer within. Even half-indifferent sightseers dropped their voices as they told a newcomer: "You see that carriage over there? That's Mrs. Alexander. They haven't found him yet. She got off the train this morning. Horton met her. She heard it in Boston yesterday--heard the newsboys crying it in the street."

At noon Philip Horton made his way through the crowd with a tray and a tin coffee-pot from the camp kitchen. When he reached the carriage he found Mrs. Alexander just as he had left her in the early morning, leaning forward a little, with her hand on the lowered window, looking at the river. Hour after hour she had been watching the water, the lonely, useless stone towers, and the convulsed mass of iron wreckage over which the angry river continually spat up its yellow foam.

"Those poor women out there, do they blame him very much?" she asked, as she handed the coffee-cup back to Horton.

"Nobody blames him, Mrs. Alexander. If any one is to blame, I'm afraid it's I. I should have stopped work before he came. He said so as soon as I met him. I tried to get him here a day earlier, but my telegram missed him, somehow. He didn't have time really to explain to me. If he'd got here Monday, he'd have had all the men off at once. But, you see, Mrs. Alexander, such a thing never happened before. According to all human calculations, it simply couldn't happen."

Horton leaned wearily against the front wheel of the cab. He had not had his clothes off for thirty hours, and the stimulus of violent excitement was beginning to wear off.

"Don't be afraid to tell me the worst, Mr. Horton. Don't leave me to the dread of finding out things that people may be saying. If he is blamed, if he needs any one to speak for him,"--for the first time her voice broke and a flush of life, tearful, painful, and confused, swept over her rigid pallor,--"if he needs any one, tell me, show me what to do." She began to sob, and Horton hurried away.

When he came back at four o'clock in the afternoon he was carrying his hat in his hand, and Winifred knew as soon as she saw him that they had found Bartley. She opened the carriage door before he reached her and stepped to the ground.

Horton put out his hand as if to hold her back and spoke pleadingly: "Won't you drive up to my house, Mrs. Alexander? They will take him up there."

"Take me to him now, please. I shall not make any trouble."

The group of men down under the riverbank fell back when they saw a woman coming, and one of them threw a tarpaulin over the stretcher. They took off their hats and caps as Winifred approached, and although she had pulled her veil down over her face they did not look up at her. She was taller than Horton, and some of the men thought she was the tallest woman they had ever seen. "As tall as himself," some one whispered. Horton motioned to the men, and six of them lifted the stretcher and began to carry it up the embankment. Winifred followed them the half-mile to Horton's house. She walked quietly, without once breaking or stumbling. When the bearers put the stretcher down in Horton's spare bedroom, she thanked them and gave her hand to each in turn. The men went out of the house and through the yard with their caps in their hands. They were too much confused to say anything as they went down the hill.

Horton himself was almost as deeply perplexed. "Mamie," he said to his wife, when he came out of the spare room half an hour later, "will you take Mrs. Alexander the things she needs? She is going to do everything herself. Just stay about where you can hear her and go in if she wants you."

Everything happened as Alexander had foreseen in that moment of prescience under the river. With her own hands she washed him clean of every mark of disaster. All night he was alone with her in the still house, his great head lying deep in the pillow. In the pocket of his coat Winifred found the letter that he had written her the night before he left New York, water-soaked and illegible, but because of its length, she knew it had been meant for her.

For Alexander death was an easy creditor. Fortune, which had smiled upon him consistently all his life, did not desert him in the end. His harshest critics did not doubt that, had he lived, he would have retrieved himself. Even Lucius Wilson did not see in this accident the disaster he had once foretold.

When a great man dies in his prime there is no surgeon who can say whether he did well; whether or not the future was his, as it seemed to be. The mind that society had come to regard as a powerful and reliable machine, dedicated to its service, may for a long time have been sick within itself and bent upon its own destruction.

EPILOGUE

Professor Wilson had been living in London for six years and he was just back from a visit to America. One afternoon, soon after his return, he put on his frock-coat and drove in a hansom to pay a call upon Hilda Burgoyne, who still lived at her old number, off Bedford Square. He and Miss Burgoyne had been fast friends for a long time. He had first noticed her about the corridors of the British Museum, where he read constantly. Her being there so often had made him feel that he would like to know her, and as she was not an inaccessible person, an introduction was not difficult. The preliminaries once over, they came to depend a great deal upon each other, and Wilson, after his day's reading, often went round to Bedford Square for his tea. They had much more in common than their memories of a common friend. Indeed, they seldom spoke of him. They saved that for the deep moments which do not come often, and then their talk of him was mostly silence. Wilson knew that Hilda had loved him; more than this he had not tried to know.

It was late when Wilson reached Hilda's apartment on this particular December afternoon, and he found her alone. She sent for fresh tea and made him comfortable, as she had such a knack of making people comfortable.

"How good you were to come back before Christmas! I quite dreaded the Holidays without you. You've helped me over a good many Christmases." She smiled at him gayly.

"As if you needed me for that! But, at any rate, I needed YOU. How well you are looking, my dear, and how rested."

He peered up at her from his low chair, balancing the tips of his long fingers together in a judicial manner which had grown on him with years.

Hilda laughed as she carefully poured his cream. "That means that I was looking very seedy at the end of the season, doesn't it? Well, we must show wear at last, you know."

Wilson took the cup gratefully. "Ah, no need to remind a man of seventy, who has just been home to find that he has survived all his contemporaries. I was most gently treated--as a sort of precious relic. But, do you know, it made me feel awkward to be hanging about still."

"Seventy? Never mention it to me." Hilda looked appreciatively at the Professor's alert face, with so many kindly lines about the mouth and so many quizzical ones about the eyes. "You've got to hang about for me, you know. I can't even let you go home again. You must stay put, now that I have you back. You're the realest thing I have."

Wilson chuckled. "Dear me, am I? Out of so many conquests and the spoils of conquered cities! You've really missed me? Well, then, I shall hang. Even if you have at last to put ME in the mummy-room with the others. You'll visit me often, won't you?"

"Every day in the calendar. Here, your cigarettes are in this drawer, where you left them." She struck a match and lit one for him. "But you did, after all, enjoy being at home again?"

"Oh, yes. I found the long railway journeys trying. People live a thousand miles apart. But I did it thoroughly; I was all over the place. It was in Boston I lingered longest."

"Ah, you saw Mrs. Alexander?"

"Often. I dined with her, and had tea there a dozen different times, I should think. Indeed, it was to see her that I lingered on and on. I found that I still loved to go to the house. It always seemed as if Bartley were there, somehow, and that at any moment one might hear his heavy tramp on the stairs. Do you know, I kept feeling that he must be up in his study." The Professor looked reflectively into the grate. "I should really have liked to go up there. That was where I had my last long talk with him. But Mrs. Alexander never suggested it."

"Why?"

Wilson was a little startled by her tone, and he turned his head so quickly that his cuff-link caught the string of his nose-glasses and pulled them awry. "Why? Why, dear me, I don't know. She probably never thought of it."

Hilda bit her lip. "I don't know what made me say that. I didn't mean to interrupt. Go on please, and tell me how it was."

"Well, it was like that. Almost as if he were there. In a way, he really is there. She never lets him go. It's the most beautiful and dignified sorrow I've ever known. It's so beautiful that it has its compensations, I should think. Its very completeness is a compensation. It gives her a fixed star to steer by. She doesn't drift. We sat there evening after evening in the quiet of that magically haunted room, and watched the sunset burn on the river, and felt him. Felt him with a difference, of course."

Hilda leaned forward, her elbow on her knee, her chin on her hand. "With a difference? Because of her, you mean?"

Wilson's brow wrinkled. "Something like that, yes. Of course, as time goes on, to her he becomes more and more their simple personal relation."

Hilda studied the droop of the Professor's head intently. "You didn't altogether like that? You felt it wasn't wholly fair to him?"

Wilson shook himself and readjusted his glasses. "Oh, fair enough. More than fair. Of course, I always felt that my image of him was just a little different from hers. No relation is so complete that it can hold absolutely all of a person. And I liked him just as he was; his deviations, too; the places where he didn't square."

Hilda considered vaguely. "Has she grown much older?" she asked at last.

"Yes, and no. In a tragic way she is even handsomer. But colder. Cold for everything but him. `Forget thyself to marble'; I kept thinking of that. Her happiness was a happiness a deux, not apart from the world, but actually against it. And now her grief is like that. She saves herself for it and doesn't even go through the form of seeing people much. I'm sorry. It would be better for her, and might be so good for them, if she could let other people in."

"Perhaps she's afraid of letting him out a little, of sharing him with somebody."

Wilson put down his cup and looked up with vague alarm. "Dear me, it takes a woman to think of that, now! I don't, you know, think we ought to be hard on her. More, even, than the rest of us she didn't choose her destiny. She underwent it. And it has left her chilled. As to her not wishing to take the world into her confidence--well, it is a pretty brutal and stupid world, after all, you know."

Hilda leaned forward. "Yes, I know, I know. Only I can't help being glad that there was something for him even in stupid and vulgar people. My little Marie worshiped him. When she is dusting I always know when she has come to his picture."

Wilson nodded. "Oh, yes! He left an echo. The ripples go on in all of us. He belonged to the people who make the play, and most of us are only onlookers at the best. We shouldn't wonder too much at Mrs. Alexander. She must feel how useless it would be to stir about, that she may as well sit still; that nothing can happen to her after Bartley."

"Yes," said Hilda softly, "nothing can happen to one after Bartley."

They both sat looking into the fire.

*****

THE BARREL ORGAN by Alfred Noyes

There's a barrel-organ caroling across a golden street,
  In the City as the sun sinks low;
And the music's not immortal; but the world has made it sweet
  And fulfilled it with the sunset glow;
And it pulses through the pleasures of the City and the pain
  That surround the singing organ like a large eternal light;
And they've given it a glory and a part to play again
  In the Symphony that rules the day and the night.

And now it's marching onward through the realms of old romance,
  And trolling out a fond familiar tune,
And now it's roaring cannon down to fight the King of France,
  And now it's prattling softly to the moon,
And all around the organ there's a sea without a shore
  Of human joys and wonders and regrets;
To remember and to recompense the music evermore

For what the cold machinery forgets. . . .

Yes; as the music changes,
  Like a prismatic glass,
It takes the light and ranges
  Through all the moods that pass;
Dissects the common carnival
  Of passions and regrets,
And gives the world a glimpse of all
  The colors it forgets.

And there LA TRAVIATA sights
  Another sadder song;
And there IL TROVATORE cries
  A tale of deeper wrong;
And bolder knights to battle go
  With sword and shield and lance,
Than ever here on earth below
  Have whirled into--A DANCE!--

Go down to Kew in lilac time; in lilac time; in lilac time;
Go down to Kew in lilac time; (it isn't far from London!)
And you shall wander hand in hand with love in summer's wonderland;
Go down to Kew in lilac time; (it isn't far from London!)

The cherry-trees are seas of bloom and soft perfume and sweet perfume,
The cherry-trees are seas of bloom (and oh, so near to London!)
And there they say, when dawn is high and all the world's a blaze of sky
The cuckoo, though he's very shy, will sing a song for London.

The nightingale is rather rare and yet they say you'll hear him there
At Kew, at Kew in lilac time (and oh, so near to London!)
The linnet and the throstle, too, and after dark the long halloo

And golden-eyed TU-WHIT, TU WHOO of owls that ogle London.

For Noah hardly knew a bird of any kind that isn't heard
At Kew, at Kew in lilac time (and oh, so near to London!)
And when the rose begins to pout and all the chestnut spires are out
You'll hear the rest without a doubt, all chorusing for London:--

COME DOWN TO KEW IN LILAC TIME; IN LILAC TIME; IN LILAC TIME;
COME DOWN TO KEW IN LILAC TIME; (IT ISN'T FAR FROM LONDON!)
 AND YOU SHALL WANDER HAND IN HAND WITH LOVE IN SUMMER'S
WONDERLAND;
 COME DOWN TO KEW IN LILAC TIME; (IT ISN'T FAR FROM LONDON!)

And then the troubadour begins to thrill the golden street,
  In the City as the sun sinks low;
And in all the gaudy busses there are scores of weary feet
Marking time, sweet time, with a dull mechanic beat,
And a thousand hearts are plunging to a love they'll never meet,
Through the meadows of the sunset, through the poppies and the wheat,
  In the land where the dead dreams go.

Verdi, Verdi, when you wrote IL TROVATORE did you dream
  Of the City when the sun sinks low
Of the organ and the monkey and the many-colored stream
On the Piccadilly pavement, of the myriad eyes that seem
To be litten for a moment with a wild Italian gleam
As A CHE LA MORTE parodies the world's eternal theme
  And pulses with the sunset glow?

There's a thief, perhaps, that listens with a face of frozen stone
  In the City as the sun sinks low;
There's a portly man of business with a balance of his own,
There's a clerk and there's a butcher of a soft reposeful tone,

And they're all them returning to the heavens they have known:
They are crammed and jammed in busses and--they're each of them alone
  In the land where the dead dreams go.

There's a very modish woman and her smile is very bland
  In the City as the sun sinks low;
And her hansom jingles onward, but her little jeweled hand
Is clenched a little tighter and she cannot understand
What she wants or why she wanders to that undiscovered land,
For the parties there are not at all the sort of thing she planned,
  In the land where the dead dreams go.

There's an Oxford man that listens and his heart is crying out
  In the City as the sun sinks low;
For the barge the eight, the Isis, and the coach's whoop and shout,
For the minute gun, the counting and the long disheveled rout,
For the howl along the tow-path and a fate that's still in doubt,
For a roughened oar to handle and a race to think about
  In the land where the dead dreams go.

There's a laborer that listen to the voices of the dead
  In the City as the sun sinks low;
And his hand begins to tremble and his face is rather red
As he sees a loafer watching him and--there he turns his head
And stares into the sunset where his April love is fled,
For he hears her softly singing and his lonely soul is led
  Through the land where the dead dreams go.

There's and old and hardened demi-rep, it's ringing in her ears,
  In the City as the sun sinks low;
With the wild and empty sorrow of the love that blights and sears,
Oh, and if she hurries onward, then be sure, be sure she hears,
Hears and bears the bitter burden of the unforgotten years,

And her laugh's a little harsher and her eyes are brimmed with tears
  For the land where the dead dreams go.

There's a barrel-organ caroling across a golden street,
  In the City as the sun sinks low;
Though the music's only Verdi there's a world to make it sweet
Just as yonder yellow sunset where the earth and heaven meet
Mellows all the sooty City! Hark, a hundred thousand feet
Are marching on to glory through the poppies and the wheat
  In the land where the dead dreams go.

        So it's Jeremiah, Jeremiah,
          What have you to say
        When you meet the garland girls
          Tripping on their way?

        All around my gala hat
          I wear a wreath of roses
        (A long and lonely year it is
          I've waited for the May!)

        If any one should ask you,
          The reason why I wear it is,
        My own love, my true love, is coming home to-day.

It's buy a bunch of violets for the lady
  (IT'S LILAC TIME IN LONDON; IT'S LILAC TIME IN LONDON!)
Buy a bunch of violets for the lady;
  While the sky burns blue above:

On the other side of the street you'll find it shady
  (IT'S LILAC TIME IN LONDON; IT'S LILAC TIME IN LONDON!)
But buy a bunch of violets for the lady;

And tell her she's your own true love.

There's a barrel-organ caroling across a golden street,
  In the City as the sun sinks glittering and slow;
And the music's not immortal, but the world has made it sweet
And enriched it with the harmonies that make a song complete
In the deeper heavens of music where the night and morning meet,
  As it dies into the sunset glow;

And it pulses through the pleasures of the City and the pain
  That surround the singing organ like a large eternal light,
And they've given it a glory and a part of play again
  In the Symphony that rules the day and night.

     And there, as the music changes,
       The song runs round again;
     Once more it turns and ranges
       Through all its joy and pain:
     Dissects the common carnival
       Of passions and regrets;
     And the wheeling world remembers all
       The wheeling song forgets.

     Once more La TRAVIATA sighs
       Another sadder song:
     Once more IL TROVATORE cries
       A tale of deeper wrong;
     Once more the knights to battle go
       With sword and shield and lance,
     Till once, once more, the shattered foe
       Has whirled into--A DANCE--

Come down to Kew in lilac time; in lilac time; in lilac time;

Come down to Kew in lilac time; (it isn't far from London!)
And you shall wander hand in hand with Love in summer's wonderland;
Come down to Kew in lilac time; (it isn't far from London!)

COME DOWN TO KEW IN LILAC TIME; IN LILAC TIME; IN LILAC TIME;
COME DOWN TO KEW IN LILAC TIME; (IT ISN'T FAR FROM LONDON!)
 AND YOU SHALL WANDER HAND IN HAND WITH LOVE IN SUMMER'S
WONDERLAND;
COME DOWN TO KEW IN LILAC TIME; (IT ISN'T FAR FROM LONDON!)

The Codes Of Hammurabi And Moses
W. W. Davies

The discovery of the Hammurabi Code is one of the greatest achievements of archaeology, and is of paramount interest, not only to the student of the Bible, but also to all those interested in ancient history...

Religion   **ISBN:** *1-59462-338-4*   **Pages:132**

MSRP $12.95

QTY

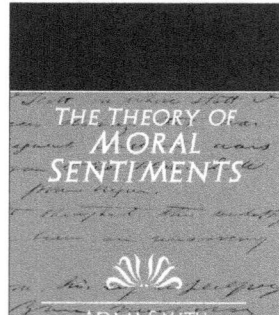

The Theory of Moral Sentiments
Adam Smith

This work from 1749. contains original theories of conscience amd moral judgment and it is the foundation for systemof morals.

Philosophy   **ISBN:** *1-59462-777-0*   **Pages:536**

MSRP $19.95

QTY

Jessica's First Prayer
Hesba Stretton

In a screened and secluded corner of one of the many railway-bridges which span the streets of London there could be seen a few years ago, from five o'clock every morning until half past eight, a tidily set-out coffee-stall, consisting of a trestle and board, upon which stood two large tin cans, with a small fire of charcoal burning under each so as to keep the coffee boiling during the early hours of the morning when the work-people were thronging into the city on their way to their daily toil...

Childrens   **ISBN:** *1-59462-373-2*   **Pages:84**

MSRP $9.95

QTY

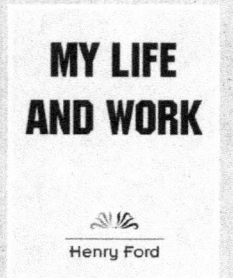

My Life and Work
Henry Ford

Henry Ford revolutionized the world with his implementation of mass production for the Model T automobile. Gain valuable business insight into his life and work with his own auto-biography... "We have only started on our development of our country we have not as yet, with all our talk of wonderful progress, done more than scratch the surface. The progress has been wonderful enough but..."

Biographies/   **ISBN:** *1-59462-198-5*   **Pages:300**

MSRP $21.95

QTY

The Art of Cross-Examination
Francis Wellman

QTY

I presume it is the experience of every author, after his first book is published upon an important subject, to be almost overwhelmed with a wealth of ideas and illustrations which could readily have been included in his book, and which to his own mind, at least, seem to make a second edition inevitable. Such certainly was the case with me; and when the first edition had reached its sixth impression in five months, I rejoiced to learn that it seemed to my publishers that the book had met with a sufficiently favorable reception to justify a second and considerably enlarged edition. ..

Reference   ISBN: *1-59462-647-2*

Pages:412

MSRP $19.95

On the Duty of Civil Disobedience
Henry David Thoreau

QTY

Thoreau wrote his famous essay, On the Duty of Civil Disobedience, as a protest against an unjust but popular war and the immoral but popular institution of slave-owning. He did more than write—he declined to pay his taxes, and was hauled off to gaol in consequence. Who can say how much this refusal of his hastened the end of the war and of slavery ?

Law   ISBN: *1-59462-747-9*

Pages:48

MSRP $7.45

Dream Psychology Psychoanalysis for Beginners
Sigmund Freud

QTY

Sigmund Freud, born Sigismund Schlomo Freud (May 6, 1856 - September 23, 1939), was a Jewish-Austrian neurologist and psychiatrist who co-founded the psychoanalytic school of psychology. Freud is best known for his theories of the unconscious mind, especially involving the mechanism of repression; his redefinition of sexual desire as mobile and directed towards a wide variety of objects; and his therapeutic techniques, especially his understanding of transference in the therapeutic relationship and the presumed value of dreams as sources of insight into unconscious desires.

Dream Psychology
Psychoanalysis for Beginners

Sigmund Freud

Psychology   ISBN: *1-59462-905-6*

Pages:196

MSRP $15.45

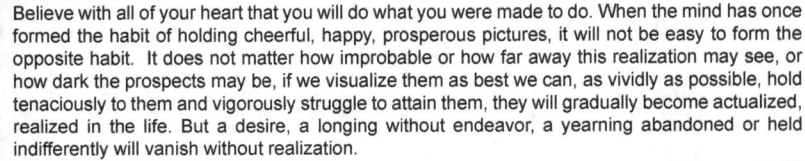

The Miracle of Right Thought
Orison Swett Marden

QTY

Believe with all of your heart that you will do what you were made to do. When the mind has once formed the habit of holding cheerful, happy, prosperous pictures, it will not be easy to form the opposite habit. It does not matter how improbable or how far away this realization may see, or how dark the prospects may be, if we visualize them as best we can, as vividly as possible, hold tenaciously to them and vigorously struggle to attain them, they will gradually become actualized, realized in the life. But a desire, a longing without endeavor, a yearning abandoned or held indifferently will vanish without realization.

Pages:360

Self Help   ISBN: *1-59462-644-8*

MSRP $25.45

www.bookjungle.com *email: sales@bookjungle.com fax: 630-214-0564 mail: Book Jungle PO Box 2226 Champaign, IL 61825*

QTY

The Rosicrucian Cosmo-Conception Mystic Christianity *by Max Heindel*　ISBN: *1-59462-188-8*　**$38.95**
The Rosicrucian Cosmo-conception is not dogmatic, neither does it appeal to any other authority than the reason of the student. It is: not controversial, but is: sent forth in the, hope that it may help to clear...　New Age/Religion Pages 646

Abandonment To Divine Providence *by Jean-Pierre de Caussade*　ISBN: *1-59462-228-0*　**$25.95**
"The Rev. Jean Pierre de Caussade was one of the most remarkable spiritual writers of the Society of Jesus in France in the 18th Century. His death took place at Toulouse in 1751. His works have gone through many editions and have been republished...　Inspirational/Religion Pages 400

Mental Chemistry *by Charles Haanel*　ISBN: *1-59462-192-6*　**$23.95**
Mental Chemistry allows the change of material conditions by combining and appropriately utilizing the power of the mind. Much like applied chemistry creates something new and unique out of careful combinations of chemicals the mastery of mental chemistry...　New Age Pages 354

The Letters of Robert Browning and Elizabeth Barret Barrett 1845-1846 vol II　ISBN: *1-59462-193-4*　**$35.95**
by Robert Browning and Elizabeth Barrett　Biographies Pages 596

Gleanings In Genesis (volume I) *by Arthur W. Pink*　ISBN: *1-59462-130-6*　**$27.45**
Appropriately has Genesis been termed "the seed plot of the Bible" for in it we have, in germ form, almost all of the great doctrines which are afterwards fully developed in the books of Scripture which follow...　Religion/Inspirational Pages 420

The Master Key *by L. W. de Laurence*　ISBN: *1-59462-001-6*　**$30.95**
In no branch of human knowledge has there been a more lively increase of the spirit of research during the past few years than in the study of Psychology, Concentration and Mental Discipline. The requests for authentic lessons in Thought Control, Mental Discipline and...　New Age/Business Pages 422

The Lesser Key Of Solomon Goetia *by L. W. de Laurence*　ISBN: *1-59462-092-X*　**$9.95**
This translation of the first book of the "Lernegton" which is now for the first time made accessible to students of Talismanic Magic was done, after careful collation and edition, from numerous Ancient Manuscripts in Hebrew, Latin, and French...　New Age/Occult Pages 92

Rubaiyat Of Omar Khayyam *by Edward Fitzgerald*　ISBN:*1-59462-332-5*　**$13.95**
Edward Fitzgerald, whom the world has already learned, in spite of his own efforts to remain within the shadow of anonymity, to look upon as one of the rarest poets of the century, was born at Bredfield, in Suffolk, on the 31st of March, 1809. He was the third son of John Purcell...　Music Pages 172

Ancient Law *by Henry Maine*　ISBN: *1-59462-128-4*　**$29.95**
The chief object of the following pages is to indicate some of the earliest ideas of mankind, as they are reflected in Ancient Law, and to point out the relation of those ideas to modern thought.　Religiom/History Pages 452

Far-Away Stories *by William J. Locke*　ISBN: *1-59462-129-2*　**$19.45**
"Good wine needs no bush, but a collection of mixed vintages does. And this book is just such a collection. Some of the stories I do not want to remain buried for ever in the museum files of dead magazine-numbers an author's not unpardonable vanity..."　Fiction Pages 272

Life of David Crockett *by David Crockett*　ISBN: *1-59462-250-7*　**$27.45**
"Colonel David Crockett was one of the most remarkable men of the times in which he lived. Born in humble life, but gifted with a strong will, an indomitable courage, and unremitting perseverance...　Biographies/New Age Pages 424

Lip-Reading *by Edward Nitchie*　ISBN: *1-59462-206-X*　**$25.95**
Edward B. Nitchie, founder of the New York School for the Hard of Hearing, now the Nitchie School of Lip-Reading, Inc, wrote "LIP-READING Principles and Practice". The development and perfecting of this meritorious work on lip-reading was an undertaking...　How-to Pages 400

A Handbook of Suggestive Therapeutics, Applied Hypnotism, Psychic Science　ISBN: *1-59462-214-0*　**$24.95**
by Henry Munro　Health/New Age/Health/Self-help Pages 376

A Doll's House: and Two Other Plays *by Henrik Ibsen*　ISBN: *1-59462-112-8*　**$19.95**
Henrik Ibsen created this classic when in revolutionary 1848 Rome. Introducing some striking concepts in playwriting for the realist genre, this play has been studied the world over.　Fiction/Classics/Plays 308

The Light of Asia *by sir Edwin Arnold*　ISBN: *1-59462-204-3*　**$13.95**
In this poetic masterpiece, Edwin Arnold describes the life and teachings of Buddha. The man who was to become known as Buddha to the world was born as Prince Gautama of India but he rejected the worldly riches and abandoned the reigns of power when... Religion/History/Biographies Pages 170

The Complete Works of Guy de Maupassant *by Guy de Maupassant*　ISBN: *1-59462-157-8*　**$16.95**
"For days and days, nights and nights, I had dreamed of that first kiss which was to consecrate our engagement, and I knew not on what spot I should put my lips..."　Fiction/Classics Pages 240

The Art of Cross-Examination *by Francis L. Wellman*　ISBN: *1-59462-309-0*　**$26.95**
Written by a renowned trial lawyer, Wellman imparts his experience and uses case studies to explain how to use psychology to extract desired information through questioning.　How-to/Science/Reference Pages 408

Answered or Unanswered? *by Louisa Vaughan*　ISBN: *1-59462-248-5*　**$10.95**
Miracles of Faith in China　Religion Pages 112

The Edinburgh Lectures on Mental Science (1909) *by Thomas*　ISBN: *1-59462-008-3*　**$11.95**
This book contains the substance of a course of lectures recently given by the writer in the Queen Street Hail, Edinburgh. Its purpose is to indicate the Natural Principles governing the relation between Mental Action and Material Conditions...　New Age/Psychology Pages 148

Ayesha *by H. Rider Haggard*　ISBN: *1-59462-301-5*　**$24.95**
Verily and indeed it is the unexpected that happens! Probably if there was one person upon the earth from whom the Editor of this, and of a certain previous history, did not expect to hear again...　Classics Pages 380

Ayala's Angel *by Anthony Trollope*　ISBN: *1-59462-352-X*　**$29.95**
The two girls were both pretty, but Lucy who was twenty-one who supposed to be simple and comparatively unattractive, whereas Ayala was credited, as her Bombwhat romantic name might show, with poetic charm and a taste for romance. Ayala when her father died was nineteen...　Fiction Pages 484

The American Commonwealth *by James Bryce*　ISBN: *1-59462-286-8*　**$34.45**
An interpretation of American democratic political theory. It examines political mechanics and society from the perspective of Scotsman James Bryce　Politics Pages 572

Stories of the Pilgrims *by Margaret P. Pumphrey*　ISBN: *1-59462-116-0*　**$17.95**
This book explores pilgrims religious oppression in England as well as their escape to Holland and eventual crossing to America on the Mayflower, and their early days in New England...　History Pages 268

QTY

The Fasting Cure *by Sinclair Upton*   ISBN: *1-59462-222-1*   **$13.95**
In the Cosmopolitan Magazine for May, 1910, and in the Contemporary Review (London) for April, 1910, I published an article dealing with my experi-ences in fasting. I have written a great many magazine articles, but never one which attracted so much attention...   New Age/Self Help/Health Pages 164

Hebrew Astrology *by Sepharial*   ISBN: *1-59462-308-2*   **$13.45**
In these days of advanced thinking it is a matter of common observation that we have left many of the old landmarks behind and that we are now pressing forward to greater heights and to a wider horizon than that which represented the mind-content of our progenitors...   Astrology Pages 144

Thought Vibration or The Law of Attraction in the Thought World   ISBN: *1-59462-127-6*   **$12.95**

by William Walker Atkinson   *Psychology/Religion Pages 144*

Optimism *by Helen Keller*   ISBN: *1-59462-108-X*   **$15.95**
Helen Keller was blind, deaf, and mute since 19 months old, yet famously learned how to overcome these handicaps, communicate with the world, and spread her lectures promoting optimism. An inspiring read for everyone...   Biographies/Inspirational Pages 84

Sara Crewe *by Frances Burnett*   ISBN: *1-59462-360-0*   **$9.45**
In the first place, Miss Minchin lived in London. Her home was a large, dull, tall one, in a large, dull square, where all the houses were alike, and all the sparrows were alike, and where all the door-knockers made the same heavy sound...   Childrens/Classic Pages 88

The Autobiography of Benjamin Franklin *by Benjamin Franklin*   ISBN: *1-59462-135-7*   **$24.95**
The Autobiography of Benjamin Franklin has probably been more extensively read than any other American historical work, and no other book of its kind has had such ups and downs of fortune. Franklin lived for many years in England, where he was agent...   Biographies/History Pages 332

Name	
Email	
Telephone	
Address	
City, State ZIP	

☐ **Credit Card**   ☐ **Check / Money Order**

Credit Card Number	
Expiration Date	
Signature	

Please Mail to: Book Jungle
PO Box 2226
Champaign, IL 61825
or Fax to: 630-214-0564

ORDERING INFORMATION

web*: www.bookjungle.com*
email*: sales@bookjungle.com*
fax*: 630-214-0564*
mail*: Book Jungle PO Box 2226 Champaign, IL 61825*
or PayPal *to sales@bookjungle.com*

Please contact us for bulk discounts

DIRECT-ORDER TERMS

20% Discount if You Order
Two or More Books
Free Domestic Shipping!
Accepted: Master Card, Visa,
Discover, American Express